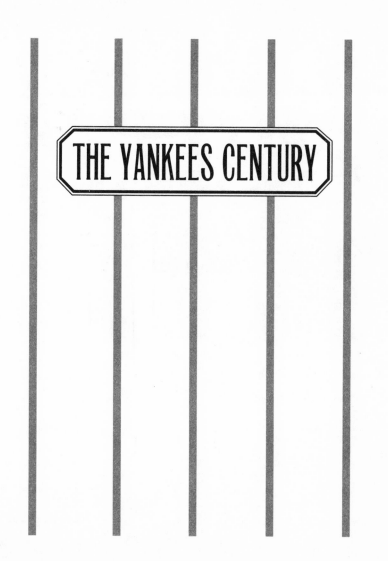

THE YANKEES CENTURY

THE YANKEES CENTURY

ALAN ROSS

VOICES AND MEMORIES OF THE PINSTRIPE PAST

CUMBERLAND HOUSE
Nashville, Tennessee

Copyright © 2001 by Alan Ross.

Published by
  CUMBERLAND HOUSE PUBLISHING, INC.
  431 Harding Industrial Drive
  Nashville, Tennessee 37211
  www.CumberlandHouse.com

Cover design by Gore Studio, Nashville, Tennessee

Library of Congress Cataloging-in-Publication Data

Ross, Alan.
    The Yankees century : voices and memories of the pinstripe past
/ Alan Ross.
          p.   cm.
    Includes bibliographical references and index.
    ISBN 1-58182-198-0 (pbk. : alk. paper)
    1. New York Yankees (Baseball team)—quotations. I. Title.
GV875.N4 R66 2001
796.357'64'097471—dc21

                                        00-065774

Printed in the United States of America

2 3 4 5 6 7 8—05 04 03 02

for Karol

thank you for your most beautiful
contribution to my life

CONTENTS

INTRODUCTION

A FRIEND once asked me if I had ever seen the great Joe DiMaggio.

"Does an Old-Timers game count?"

He assured me that it did.

In that case, I consider myself fortunate to have seen the legendary Yankee Clipper in action. It was approximately twelve to thirteen seasons after his retirement in 1951, and although his head was significantly graying, Joltin' Joe stroked a double on a rope to left-center that clearly gave a hint to the power that once lurked there in his prime.

It's DiMag and Yogi, Casey and The Mick, Reggie and Thurman, Bernie and Jeter, and the overwhelming galaxy of timeless stars that ultimately brought the Yankees century into being. It is a compendium of the men in pinstripes as told, mainly, through the voices of players, coaches, managers, opponents, and sportswriters—a living retrospective on sport's greatest ongoing phenomenon: the Bronx Bombers.

If recollection of the numberless heroes in Yankee navy blue and white stirs the innards of your soul, read on.

It's all pinstripe.

I'd like to thank Ron Pitkin, Ed Curtis, Julie Jayne, and the rest of the staff of Cumberland House for their superb editorial, production, and marketing performance under an impossible gun.

Special thanks to my brother, Bob, the greatest Yankees fan in the world.

REMEMBRANCE

IT WAS a spring afternoon in 1952 when I first met Yankee Stadium. The old Yankee Stadium. The one with the turquoise-colored art-deco copper-frieze facade that rimmed the roofline from the grandstand in left field all the way around to right—a sublime vision worthy of gawking.

Yes, I too had the Billy Crystal my-father-took-me-to-my-first-big-league-ball-game-at-Yankee-Stadium-I-was-shocked-by-how-green-the-grass-was experience when I was seven.

It's amazing what you remember: My parents and I sat in a box just to the left of home plate (I thought at the time they were lousy seats because you had to look through the wire screen to see the action). I can still see Hank Bauer, the Yankees right fielder, racing around third in bright sunlight and barreling home into the long shadows that reached out from behind home plate to the infield grass and scoring on a single from second.

The opponent that day was the Philadelphia Athletics—they of Connie Mack lore and the future Kansas City-Oakland A's. I still vividly recall Athletics first baseman Ferris Fain popping up to the infield and throwing his bat in disgust, end over end, high into the sky. I gaped. It looked like the bat went higher than the ball. One more item of note: The Yanks, of course, took a 2-0 win.

There would be other trips to the hallowed Mecca of Bronx Bomberdom. Other days when a Moose Skowron home run barely curled around the right-field flagpole in the lower stands. Other times to be thrilled by an opposite-field golfed homer by The Mick. And there was that rare double-header win by pitcher Johnny Kucks.

It all translates to the heartthrob of youth—me and my Yankees.

I was lucky. I didn't just get to hear or read about my heroes—Berra, Ford, Mantle, Bauer, Martin, Rizzuto, Reynolds, Lopat, Raschi. I actually got to see them: Mantle, head bowed, trotting in from center field. Swarthy Yogi taking off his catcher's mask. Both of them returning to the dugout after an inning's work in the field. Those moments go beyond treasure, and I feel the circle turning as others before me doubtless felt upon viewing Ruth, Gehrig, Meusel, Gómez, Dickey, DiMaggio, Henrich. Haunting apparitions to later generations of fans, but larger than life for those who witnessed them on the field.

And through it all there has been one constant—the magnificent stadium. The grand overseer. The guardian of the magic. The keeper of the pinstripes.

1

PINSTRIPE TRADITION

The myth of the Yankee pinstripe, which insisted that merely putting on the Yankee uniform made you part of a remorseless, invincible team, did not yet exist. The 1927 club carved out its beginnings.

John Mosedale
writer and author

THE PLAYERS, the stadium, the pinstripes, "five o'clock lightning," the innumerable Yankee come-from-behind wins, the legend that transcends myth. Blend it all together and you have a twenty-six-time world champion. That's over one quarter of the ninety-six championships played in this past century.

Some teams—Brooklyn-Los Angeles, Oakland, and Cincinnati come to mind—are fortunate to have had one dynasty in their franchise's history. Some teams never even field one. The Yankees have had five. Five separate dynasties. Imagine!

No greater tradition ever existed.

The essence of the Yankees is that they win. From in front or from behind, they win. And that's why the history of the New York Yankees is virtually the history of baseball.

Dave Anderson
The New York Times

When we were challenged, when we had to win, we stuck together and played with a fury and determination that could only come from team spirit. We had a pride in our performance that was very real. It took on the form of snobbery. We felt we were superior people, and I do believe we left a heritage that became a Yankee tradition.

Waite Hoyt
pitcher (1921–30)

Just putting on a Yankee uniform gave me a little confidence, I think. That club could carry you. You were better than you actually were.

Mark Koenig
shortstop (1925–30)

To be a Yankee is a thought in everyone's head. . . . Just walking into Yankee Stadium, chills run through you. I believe there was a higher offer, but no matter how much money is offered, if you want to be a Yankee, you don't think about it.

Jim "Catfish" Hunter
pitcher (1975–79), on his heralded free agency signing, New Year's Eve 1974

If you saw that Yankees pitching too often, there would be a lot of guys doing different jobs.

Joe Rudi
Oakland A's outfielder

Five o'clock lightning," once phrased by Earle Combs and referring to the team's ability to strike so often in the late innings, caught on, spread through the league and seeped into the consciousness of opposing pitchers. They began to dread the approach of five o'clock and the eighth inning.

Frank Graham
legendary sportswriter

When you go to other parks, they hang banners for the wild-card or Eastern Division or Western Division champions. Around here, they don't hang anything unless its for being world champions.

Chili Davis
outfielder-designated hitter
(1998–99)

Even though I have loyalty to people, you have to be loyal to twenty-five players as opposed to just one.

Joe Torre
manager (1996–)

When the Yankees came to town, it was like Barnum and Bailey coming to town . . . it was the excitement. They had these gray uniforms, but there was a blue hue to them. I'll never forget them. Watching them warm up was as exciting as watching the game. Being in Cleveland, you couldn't root for them, but you could boo them in awe.

George Steinbrenner
on growing up in Cleveland

The Yankees will never be beaten. They will only wear out.

New York Sun, 1927

THE TWENTY-SIX
WORLD SERIES CHAMPIONSHIPS

1923	v. New York Giants	4-2
1927	v. Pittsburgh Pirates	4-0
1928	v. St. Louis Cardinals	4-0
1932	v. Chicago Cubs	4-0
1936	v. New York Giants	4-2
1937	v. New York Giants	4-1
1938	v. Chicago Cubs	4-0
1939	v. Cincinnati Reds	4-0
1941	v. Brooklyn Dodgers	4-1
1943	v. St. Louis Cardinals	4-1
1947	v. Brooklyn Dodgers	4-3
1949	v. Brooklyn Dodgers	4-1
1950	v. Philadelphia Phillies	4-0
1951	v. New York Giants	4-2
1952	v. Brooklyn Dodgers	4-3
1953	v. Brooklyn Dodgers	4-2
1956	v. Brooklyn Dodgers	4-3
1958	v. Milwaukee Braves	4-3
1961	v. Cincinnati Reds	4-1
1962	v. San Francisco Giants	4-3
1977	v. Los Angeles Dodgers	4-2
1978	v. Los Angeles Dodgers	4-2
1996	v. Atlanta Braves	4-2
1998	v. San Diego Padres	4-0
1999	v. Atlanta Braves	4-0
2000	v. New York Mets	4-1

2

PINSTRIPE PRIDE

I think of myself as a Yankee.

Mark Koenig
*who, during his twelve-year
major league career, also played
with the Detroit Tigers, Chicago
Cubs, Cincinnati Reds, and
New York Giants*

EVERY MOVIEGOER of the last half-century has seen Gary Cooper's stirring portrayal of the immortal Lou Gehrig in *Pride of the Yankees*.

But the great Iron Horse wasn't the only wearer of the pinstripes to don an attitude of unbeatable pride during his Yankee days. Such first-magnitude stars as Jim "Catfish" Hunter, Reggie Jackson, and Roger Clemens all could have opted for bigger paychecks somewhere else but ultimately chose to pull on the pinstripes. A player who has achieved the stature of Clemens, with five Cy Young Awards, still wants to know the feeling of going out on top; he desires to experience the absolute ultimate before hitting retirement.

Deep down they all intuit the empirical truth: there is just nothing that beats being a Yankee.

Lou was not the best player the Yankees ever had. Ruth was number one by any yardstick, DiMaggio a more accomplished performer. Yet Lou was the most valuable player the Yankees ever had because he was a prime source of their greatest asset: an implied confidence in themselves and in every man on the club. Lou's pride as a big leaguer rubbed off on every one who played with him.

Stanley Frank

He taught us what it meant to be a Yankee.

Lefty Gómez
*pitcher (1930–42),
on Tony Lazzeri*

I'm proud to introduce the man who succeeded me in centerfield in 1951.

Joe DiMaggio
introducing Mickey Mantle to the sellout crowd at Yankee Stadium on Mickey Mantle Day, September 1965

I watched him bandage that knee—the whole leg—and I saw what he had to go through every day to play. He was taped from shin to thigh. And now I'll never be able to say enough in praise. Seeing those legs, his power becomes unbelievable.

Early Wynn
twenty-three-year major league pitcher and Hall of Famer, on Mickey Mantle, at an All-Star game in the late 1950s

When I retired I got more than fifty scrapbooks that people sent me in the mail. It gave me goose bumps to know I had that kind of effect on people. Billy Crystal did a sketch for *Saturday Night Live*, and they ran it again on *This Week in Baseball*. He's talking about how his dad took him to a game one time, and then he says, "Mick hit one out of the park. It was a good day." That's nice, really nice, to have people feel that way.

Mickey Mantle, 1994

I don't think [Casey Stengel] ever cared about your color if you wore the Yankee uniform with pride.

Elston Howard
catcher-infielder (1955–67), nine-time AL All-Star, 1963 AL MVP

Even now I look up to him, he's never disappointed me.

Andy Pafko
*seventeen-year National League
player and four-time All-Star,
on Joe DiMaggio*

For sixteen years into every ball park in which I have ever walked, I received nothing but kindness and encouragement. Mine has been a full life. . . . I have been privileged to play many years with the famous Yankees, the greatest team of all times. . . . I may have been given a bad break, but I have an awful lot to live for. All in all, I can say on this day that I consider myself the luckiest man on the face of the earth.

Lou Gehrig
*from his farewell speech on
Lou Gehrig Appreciation Day,
July 4, 1939*

I never knew how someone who was dying could say he was the luckiest man in the world. But now I understand.

Mickey Mantle
June 8, 1969, referring to Lou Gehrig's immortal farewell speech the day Mantle's No. 7 was retired at Yankee Stadium

The ghosts of Ruth and Gehrig, DiMaggio and Mantle seem to hover over the stadium, inspiring the current wearers of the sacred pinstripes with a confidence no other team can match—Yankee pride— and perhaps from time to time nudging a ball over the fence or into a glove— Yankee luck.

Kenneth Auchincloss
writer, Newsweek, October 30, 2000

If you're a Yankee fan, or if you're not a Yankee fan—you have to admit, we're winners.

Paul O'Neill
outfielder (1993–),
after the 2000 World Series

We *are* the New York Yankees.

George Steinbrenner

3

YANKEES IN PINSTRIPES

I never take this job for granted. I never lose sight of the ones who have come before me out there. It's not just Mr. DiMaggio and Mickey Mantle. You think about Bobby Murcer and Mickey Rivers. You think about the kind of center field Paul Blair played when he was a Yankee. The truth is, the best thing for me is to not think about those people too much. The best thing for me is to keep going.

Bernie Williams
center fielder

In 1998 Williams became the first player to win a batting title, Gold Glove Award, and a World Series championship in the same season. Sharing honors with switch-hitting teammate Jorge Posada, Williams is part of the only pair of teammates to hit homers from both sides of the plate in the same game

MOST EVERY follower of the Bronx Bombers can call off the roll of imposing superstars who have gained legendary status as a New York Yankee—Ruth, Gehrig, Dickey, DiMaggio, Mantle, Maris, Berra, Ford, Munson, Guidry, Jackson, Hunter, Nettles, Mattingly, Jeter.

But just below the mythical quality of these performers, a plethora of stars has always contributed to the great Yankee mosaic. Players along the level of Charley "King Kong" Keller, Spud Chandler, Joe Gordon, Tommy Henrich, Vic Raschi, Allie Reynolds, Bobby Murcer, Bobby Richardson, Tony Kubek, Joe Pepitone, Sparky Lyle, Paul O'Neill, Tino Martinez, and Bernie Williams.

Then there were the worker bees: the unsung gladiators who day in and day out toiled in relative obscurity, sometimes laboring in the massive shadow of a legend: the Mark Koenigs, the Andy Careys, the Bob Cervs, the Horace Clarkes, the Luis Sojos.

All shared one thing in common: They were every bit a Yankee.

If you were to cut that bird's head open, the weakness of every batter in the league would fall out.

Anonymous Yankee coach
on Hall of Fame pitcher
Herb Pennock (1923–33)

You didn't face a left-hander, you faced Herb Pennock.

Harry Heilmann
Hall of Famer and four-time AL
batting champion with Detroit, to
teammate Bob "Fatty" Fothergill,
who boasted that no left-hander
could get him out (Fothergill went
0 for 4 against Pennock)

Tony Lazzeri was "Poosh 'Em Up," a name dating back to his first year in organized baseball, with Salt Lake City, when he was struggling, and a restaurant owner named Tony Roffetti took pity on him, feeding him spaghetti dinners three nights running, and urging him to "poosh 'em up," meaning hit.

John Mosedale

He didn't discover America, but then Columbus never went behind third for an overthrow to cut off the tying run in the ninth inning.

The New York Times
on Tony Lazzeri

Leftfielder Bob Meusel had, by common consent, the best arm in baseball—a rifle, who also hit for the average (.315 in 1926) and with power. The only year during the 1920s that Ruth did not lead the league in home runs—1925—Meusel was the leader, with 33, and the runs-batted-in leader, too. . . . He traditionally led the league in assists for an outfielder.

John Mosedale

Babe saved the game . . . he was a wild man, so we have similar personalities. I wish I could wear number 3. I wish they could take it out of retirement. Maybe I could wear 03.

David Wells
pitcher (1997–98),
who wound up wearing number 33

There was never any more doubt about Earle Combs' athletic prowess than about his character. Of the latter, Joe McCarthy, his manager in Louisville, said, "Earle Combs is the greatest gentleman in baseball"; as to the other, Gehrig moved Joe DiMaggio over to make room in center field for Combs on his all-time Yankee team.

John Mosedale

It's all over boys. Here comes Frank Merriwell.

Dan Howley
St. Louis Browns manager, on Yankees reliever Wilcy Moore, a thirty-year-old rookie phenom in 1927, who won 19 games for New York, recording a league-high 13 saves

He has rather a spare and meager frame, when he stands with his bat poised expectantly and his thin legs somewhat apart, his body forward, he suggests a kangaroo ready for take-off. His antics in the field are also in character. The way he darts about, scooping up grounders with the full play of those long arms and legs of his reminds you of a toy jumping jack on a string.

Baseball magazine
on third baseman
"Jumping Joe" Dugan

Fellows like Ruth and Gehrig can ruin an ordinary ballplayer. They win so many games by their individual efforts that you wonder why you are in the lineup.

Joe Dugan
third baseman (1922–28)

That guy can hit me in the middle of the night, blindfolded and with two broken feet to boot.

Bob Feller
Cleveland Indians Hall of Fame pitcher (1936–56), on Tommy Henrich

Hank Bauer had a face that was once described as "looking like a clenched fist."

Maury Allen
author and long-time sportswriter for the New York Post

Meet the new manager of the New York Yankees, Charles Dillon (Casey) Stengel, one-time hard-hitting outfielder, manager of both major- and minor-league clubs, sage, wit, and gifted raconteur, as glib with the wisecrack as the late Jimmy Walker.

John Drebinger
The New York Times,
October 13, 1948

On the field he was a teacher. Off the field he was a talker.

Al Lopez
one-time rival manager of both the
Cleveland Indians and Chicago
White Sox, on Casey Stengel

Casey Stengel had more baseball brains in his little finger than any other manager I knew had in their whole body.

Tommy Holmes
*Boston Braves player under
Stengel in 1942*

Holmes once held the National League record for consecutive games with a hit (37), a mark that stood unbroken until 1978, when Pete Rose hit safely in 44 straight games

If there was any one great skill Casey had as a manager, it was knowing when to pick his spots. He didn't have a degree, but he was one of the greatest doctors of psychiatry I had ever seen.

Eddie Lopat
pitcher (1948–55)

My best pitch is anything the batter grounds, lines, or pops in the direction of Phil Rizzuto.

Vic Raschi
pitcher (1946–53)

He is the greatest shortstop I have ever seen in my entire baseball career, and I have watched some beauties. Honus Wagner was a better hitter, sure, but I've seen this kid make plays Wagner never did. If I were a retired gentleman, I would follow the Yankees around just to see Rizzuto work those miracles every day.

Casey Stengel

If we had that little squirt, we'd be out in front by ten games now.

Ted Williams
on Phil Rizzuto

That little punk—how I love 'im!

Casey Stengel
on Billy Martin

There has never been anyone like this kid. He has more speed than any slugger, and more slug than any speedster.

Casey Stengel
on Mickey Mantle

Willie Mays and I, we broke in together in 1951 and then the big question was, "Who's the best, Willie, Mick, or the Duke?" I always said, long before Henry Aaron broke Ruth's home run record, that Hank was the best ballplayer of our era. He was doing the same thing Willie and I were doing. He just wasn't doing it in New York.

Mickey Mantle

Ralph Houk is the best manager I ever played for.

Mickey Mantle

I thought Roger Maris was the one guy we needed. He always played hard. And he would plow into second base with total abandon to break up a double play. He was a complete player and he could field and throw and run.

Whitey Ford

I guess it took me a while to get smart. There are certainly many things a ballplayer can do offensively besides hitting homers.

Bobby Murcer
outfielder
(1965–66, '69–74, '79–83)

Clete Boyer was the best third baseman I've ever seen, bar none. Brooks Robinson was great. Graig Nettles was great. But Clete was a better defensive player. No one could dive to the right, backhand the ball, and throw from his knees like Clete.

Tony Kubek
shortstop (1957–65)

I think Reggie Jackson on your ball club is a part of a show of force. It's a show of power. I help to intimidate the opposition, just because I'm here. That's part of my role.

Reggie Jackson
outfielder (1977–81)

The magnitude of me, the magnitude of the instance, the magnitude of New York—it's uncomfortable, it's miserable. It's uncomfortable being me, it's uncomfortable being recognized constantly, it's uncomfortable being considered something I'm not, an idol or a monster, something hated or loved.

Reggie Jackson

He'd give you the shirt off his back. Of course, he'd call a press conference to announce it.

Jim "Catfish" Hunter
on Reggie Jackson

I'm the straw that stirs the drink.

Reggie Jackson

Ten or 20 years down the road, people will always associate Don Mattingly with the Yankees. With free agency, you don't have many players who are associated with teams anymore. But Donnie will always be remembered as a Yankee. . . . There are a few guys who, whether you're playing with them or against them, you root for them. He was one of those guys. People in baseball wanted Donnie to do well because of all he'd done and how he had done it.

Paul O'Neill

Tino Martinez is definitely the heart and soul of this team. He's actually a lot like Don Mattingly—same intensity, ready to play every day. He has a lot of Mattingly's leadership qualities.

David Cone
pitcher (1995–2000)

George Steinbrenner described him as a warrior, and I think that is a perfect fit for him. . . . Paul O'Neill is the backbone of this ballclub.

Joe Torre

The kid is dynamite. I'm not sure if there's any ceiling for him.

Joe Torre
on shortstop Derek Jeter

Derek Jeter is a great player. He didn't have to prove it this Series. He could have taken it off and I still would have thought he was a great player.

Bobby Valentine
New York Mets manager,
after Jeter was named MVP
of the 2000 World Series

All I've ever wanted to be is a Yankee. When I was a kid, I was always hoping there'd be a jersey left for me to wear with a single digit, because of all the retired numbers.

Derek Jeter
shortstop (1996–), wears No. 2

Andy Pettitte's a great pitcher. He throws that cutter and there's little you can do.

Bubba Trammell
New York Mets outfielder

You can't freeze the ball in this game. You need 27 outs and the last five or six outs are the toughest ones to get. He's been as good as I've seen.

Joe Torre
on Mariano Rivera

It's really hard to center him. It's moving two ways, and it's moving pretty quickly. It's moving forward at 90-plus, and it's moving sideways rather late and rather quickly.

Bobby Valentine
New York Mets manager,
on the fastball array
of Mariano Rivera

The kid throws too hard for us. He's too good for this league. I say we ban him from baseball.

Tom Kelly
Minnesota Twins manager,
on relief ace Mariano Rivera

I never thought I was going to get here. I was fired last year [St. Louis] and I thought that was my last stop. It's very emotional to finally get here. . . . I wish this feeling could last forever.

Joe Torre
after winning the
1996 World Series

His impact is all over this team. It's all over every player.

Darryl Strawberry
outfielder (1995–99),
on Joe Torre

I think Skip's the kind of guy who's going to go down with the guys that got him here. And as a player you love that.

Andy Pettitte
pitcher (1995–),
on Joe Torre

Joe lets players play and coaches coach.

Don Zimmer
coach (1995–)

PINSTRIPE CHARACTER

You can call it the turning point in the history of the New York Yankees.

Ed Barrow

Yankees general manager; with the Yankees dormant in next to last place in the American League, a $5,000 fine was levied against Babe Ruth for arriving late for a game in St. Louis in August 1925. Ruth had led a group of agitators on the club in defiance of manager Miller Huggins. Yankee management backed Huggins's fine—the largest ever imposed on a player in major league baseball at the time. Soon the band of reprobates, Ruth included, began to fall in line and solidify as a powerhouse team

YES, THERE is talent. There has always been talent. But the heart of Yankeedom can be summed up by the uncompromising effort, the playing-hurt-because-winning-means-more attitude that has pervaded the pinstripes throughout the last century.

It's a quality that you don't find in most players. If you have it, it moves like a wisp of smoke, in and out, encircling and permeating. It is prized by kings, philosophers, and most notably, winners. It is the key ingredient to success, and it happens that the Yankees have always had it in rich abundance.

Gehrig set his record of 2,130 consecutive games in conditions he never bothered to complain about. Late in his career, X-rays of his hands revealed 17 fractures he had let heal by themselves. He had broken every finger in both hands, some twice, and didn't mention it. Hit by a pitch that gave him a concussion that should have put him in bed for a week, he came to the park the following day and got four hits.

John Mosedale

Mantle is the only man I ever saw who was crippled who could outdo the world.

Casey Stengel

There could be a kid who may be seeing me for the first or last time. I owe him my best.

Joe DiMaggio
*asked why he always played hard,
even when a game was hopelessly
lost or already won*

I ask only one thing of my players— hustle. It doesn't take any ability to hustle.

Billy Martin
*second baseman
(1950–53, 1955–57)
manager
(1975–78, '79, '83, '85, '88)*

You can't say anything too good about Roger Maris. He ran right through a wooden fence for me at Keokuk. I thought he was out for the year, but he held the ball, came to, and got up and won the game for me with a homer in the ninth. How much hustle can a guy give you?

Jo-Jo White
*Maris's manager in the Class B
Three-I League in Keokuk, Iowa*

If you bawl your players out while they're losing, they may punch you in the nose. Do it while they're winning and they'll listen.

Casey Stengel
*on player handling, learned as a
player under New York Giants
manager John McGraw*

I have always been a great admirer of Casey Stengel. He was a great manager and showed great strength of character. I don't think anybody contributed more to baseball than Casey Stengel. He ranks right up there with Ty Cobb, Babe Ruth, and Judge Landis.

Ted Williams

He made me feel part of the club. He made me feel I was a Yankee.

Elston Howard
on Casey Stengel

It's something inside his heart that's bigger than anything. He's got the heart of a lion about to grab something.

Darryl Strawberry
on David Cone

When he goes out there, he spills his guts out.

Mel Stottlemyre
pitcher (1964–74) and
coach (1995–),
on David Cone

Every year is a different story. We struggled this year. We had tough times, and the wins didn't come easy. We played the best teams in the playoffs and we're sitting here at the end of the year. This one was a little more satisfying.

Derek Jeter
after the 2000 World Series
conquest of the New York Mets

After a season-ending meltdown where they lost their last seven games and 15 out of 18, the Yanks teetered as if standing on stilts on top of the Empire State Building. . . . They should have gained universal respect for accomplishing what few of us believed they would only a month ago.

Jon Saraceno
USA Today, October 27, 2000

They just keep coming at you. It reminds me of great fighters—heavyweights who just won't let up. They come at you and wear you down. You think, "I'm gonna get 'em," but you don't.

George Steinbrenner
on his 2000 world champions

A lot of people counted us out. We showed a lot of class and what we were made of.

Jorge Posada
catcher (1995–),
after the 2000 World Series

I really don't want to talk about me right now. This is the time of year you talk about the New York Yankees.

Paul O'Neill
*the day of the final game
of the 2000 World Series*

When you have to go through tough times, I think winning is more satisfying.

Joe Torre

When you go through things with the same core of people, you never lose faith in them. And Joe [Torre] doesn't forget. That's a credit to him and what he's brought to this team.

Paul O'Neill

You play the game to win the game, and not worry about what's on the back of the baseball card at the end of the year.

Paul O'Neill

In Cuba, there is no relief pitching. . . .
It's win or die.

**Orlando "El Duque"
Hernández**

STENGELESE & YOGI-ISMS

Yogi [Berra] is dumb like a fox. Not only on the ball field but off the field too.

Mickey Mantle

IN ITS time, baseball has birthed a wondrous gallery of unconventional oddballs, cut-up comics, and colorful characters.

Two of the sport's most unique novelties wound up on the same team at the same time, a period of twelve years—the talented and entertaining Lawrence Peter Berra and Charles Dillon Stengel. Yogi and Casey to everyone.

The gems that emanated from these two magnificent assassins of the English language have had scribes scurrying to document their every dizzying word—and even some they didn't say.

Here is a smattering of some of the delightful chin music uttered from and about baseball's two most eloquent palaverists.

He's got birds in his garret.

Wilbert Robinson
*former manager, Brooklyn
Dodgers, on the classic Stengel
bird bit, June 6, 1918*

While with Pittsburgh, a teammate of Stengel's, Leon Cadore, saw a bird hit a brick wall in the Pirates' bullpen during pregame warmups at Ebbets Field. Cadore picked up the stunned bird and placed it under Stengel's cap. Stengel left it there. As the lead-off batter in the second inning, Stengel, an ex-Dodger player, was booed lustily by Dodger fans as he stepped up to the plate. In a gesture that has become legend, Stengel grandly doffed his cap to the crowd, which gasped as the bird took flight.

The 75 World Series games and the other records are not what make Yogi different. Yogi is what makes Yogi different. We had breakfast one time, and he looked at the menu and said, "I only have eggs in Cincinnati." I didn't ask him why, but you can bet he had a good reason.

Joe DiMaggio
*center fielder (1936–42;
1946–51), 13-time American
League All-Star, 3-time AL MVP*

It gets late early out there.

Yogi Berra
*on Yankee Stadium's left field,
the sun field*

Late afternoon shadows and the low-setting sun just above the facade behind first base create trying conditions for left fielders

It ain't over till it's over.

Yogi Berra

You can observe a lot by watching.

Yogi Berra

If you come to a fork in the road, take it.

Yogi Berra

Why buy good luggage? You only use it when you travel.

Yogi Berra

The future ain't what it used to be.

Yogi Berra

I never coulda done it without my players.

Casey Stengel
after winning the 1949 American League pennant in his debut season as the Yanks manager

We had this left-hander, Gazzara [Bob Kuzava] and they had that brilliant Mr. Rob-A-Son at the plate and all of a sudden, whoops, here comes a slow ball when you expect a fastball, and why wouldn't you tap it into right field if you wuz right-handed, but Mr. Rob-A-Son tried to hit the ball over the building and instead he hit a ball up the shoot . . . and Mr. Collins, which was my first baseman, was counting his money so he never seen it, and Mr. Berra, my catcher, is standing with his hands on his hips yelling for Mr. Collins, and Mr. Gazzara did the pitching and he ain't about to do the catchin', so that leaves the second baseman, and you know who that is, to come in, lose his cap, and get it before it hits the grass, which if he did would be kicked because he was runnin' so fast and almost tripped over the mound which was a mountain in Brooklyn to help them sinker ball pitchers, Mr. [Carl] Erskine and them, and McGraw used to do that too, and why wouldn't ya, if you had spitters on the staff, but my rooster caught it and it didn't hit off his schnozz like a lot of them would have.

Casey Stengel
*on Billy Martin's two-out
seventh-inning infield catch
against the Brooklyn Dodgers
to save a 4-2 Yankees win in
Game 7 of the 1952 World Series*

I remember Casey way back. As early as 1925, he was talking Stengelese. It helped sell tickets.

Ken Smith
*former newspaperman and director
of baseball's Hall of Fame*

Brooklyn was the borough of churches
and bad ball clubs, many of which I had.

Casey Stengel
*when he managed the
Brooklyn Dodgers (1934–36)*

A nickel ain't worth a dime anymore.

Yogi Berra

It's déjà vu all over again.

Yogi Berra

I ain't in no slump . . . I just ain't hitting.

Yogi Berra

Bill Dickey is learning me his experience.

Yogi Berra
as a rookie in 1946

Ninety percent of the game is half mental.

Yogi Berra

Never answer an anonymous letter.

Yogi Berra

I didn't really say everything I said.

Yogi Berra

Whenever I decided to release a guy, I always had his room searched first for a gun. You couldn't take any chances with those birds.

Casey Stengel

I had many years that I was not successful as a ballplayer, as it is a game of skill. And then I was no doubt discharged by baseball in which I had to go back to the minor leagues as a manager, and after being in the minor leagues as a manager, I became a major league manager in several cities and was discharged; we call it discharged because there is no question I had to leave.

Casey Stengel
*at the 1958 Senate subcommittee
hearings investigating baseball's
reserve clause*

Ruth, Gehrig, Huggins, someone throw that damn ball in here, now!

Casey Stengel

after a ball hit to deep center field in old Yankee Stadium rattled around the in-the-field-of-play stone monuments of Ruth, Gehrig, and Huggins, giving the center fielder fits

I know'd you'd wanna check that so I looked it up. Why wouldn't ya use all the ones you got if ya needed hitting especially since my own fellas which is new and how do you know what they can do if they hadn't played a game for ya since it don't count yet and they don't get paid.

Casey Stengel

asked to evaluate his Yankee pitching staff in the spring of 1950

They examined all my organs. Some of them are quite remarkable, and others are not so good. A lot of museums are bidding for them.

Casey Stengel
upon his release from Lenox Hill Hospital after a virus and high fever in May 1960

I commenced winning pennants when I came here, but I didn't commence getting any younger. . . . I'll never make the mistake of being 70 again.

Casey Stengel
at his Yankees resignation-discharge press conference, October 18, 1960

Just because your legs is dead doesn't mean your head is too.

Casey Stengel
at 71

Some people my age are dead at the present time.

Casey Stengel

Can't anybody play this game!

Casey Stengel

The Yankees Managers

1901–2	John McGraw	1966–73	Ralph Houk
1902	Wilbert Robinson	1974–75	Bill Virdon
1903–8	Clark Griffith	1975–78	Billy Martin
1908	Kid Elberfeld	1978–79	Bob Lemon
1909–10	George Stallings	1979	Billy Martin
1910–11	Hal Chase	1980	Dick Howser
1912	Harry Wolverton	1981	Gene Michael
1913–14	Frank Chance	1981–82	Bob Lemon
1914	Roger Peckinpaugh	1982	Gene Michael
1915–17	Bill Donovan	1982	Clyde King
1918–29	Miller Huggins	1983	Billy Martin
1929	Art Fletcher	1984–85	Yogi Berra
1930	Bob Shawkey	1985	Billy Martin
1931–46	Joe McCarthy	1986–88	Lou Pinella
1946	Bill Dickey	1988	Billy Martin
1946	Johnny Neun	1989	Dallas Green
1947–48	Bucky Harris	1989–90	Bucky Dent
1949–60	Casey Stengel	1990–91	Stump Merrill
1961–63	Ralph Houk	1992–95	Buck Showalter
1964	Yogi Berra	1996–	Joe Torre
1965–66	Johnny Keane		

6

PINSTRIPE LEGENDS

Some 20 years ago, I stopped talking about the Babe for the simple reason that I realized that those who had never seen him didn't believe me.

Tommy Holmes
eleven-year National League
outfielder (1942–52)

To understand him, you had to understand this: He wasn't human. No human could have done the things he did and lived the way he lived and been a ballplayer. Cobb? Could he pitch? Speaker? The rest? I saw them. I was there. There was never anybody close. When you figure the things he did and the way he lived and the way he played, you got to figure he was more than animal even. There was never anyone like him. He was a god.

Joe Dugan
on Babe Ruth

It was figured that Ruth would hit home runs, but when he shocked baseball by hitting 59 in 1921, it was believed that the mark would last, in baseball time, forever.

John Mosedale

Ruth was a liberator who endeavored by personal example to show that no fun ever hurt you and that a bold spirit walks through the gloom ignoring old signposts, following instead his nose, a man uncorrupted by good living.

Heywood Broun

Wasn't the Babe Sir Lancelot riding down Broadway wearing a camel's hair coat with a big cigar stuck in his mouth? Didn't he pick baseball up by the boot straps when it was rocked to the very foundation by the Black Sox Scandal? . . . People used to say they'd rather see him strike out with that tremendous flourish of his than see others knock the ball out of the park.

George Girsch
New York Daily Mirror

Babe Ruth had been a great pitcher,
capable of making the Hall of Fame
through that arduous calling alone,
having once, as every schoolboy learns
along with the pledge of allegiance,
pitched 29⅔ scoreless World Series
innings, a record that stood for 43 years.
He had become an outfielder only because
his bat was too explosive to leave out of
the daily lineup, but he retained his
marvelous arm, so that he never made a
mechanical error, never threw to the
wrong base.

John Mosedale

Sportswriters vied with one another to invent new nicknames for the Babe. One of the first had Italian origins—"The Bambino." It fit. Others were the "Behemoth of Bust," the "Rajah of Rap," the "Caliph of Clout," the "Maharajah of Mash," the "Wazir of Wham," and, of course, the "Sultan of Swat." His teammates simply called him "Jidge" or "Jidgie"—short for "George"—and he called most of them "Keed," since he could never remember their names.

Jay David

You'll never find out the whole truth about Babe Ruth. I wrote two books about him myself, and I know.

Dan Daniel

long-time sportswriter for the New York World Telegram

Only seven players have hit more than 40 home runs in a year, and Ruth is five of them.

Anonymous, 1927

The fans applauded Ruth's home run. That's his business. Not so Gehrig's. He's just a first baseman.

New York Herald Tribune
April 1927, Philadelphia
Athletics' home opener

Ruth had hit his second home run of the year, in which he would ultimately hit 60; Gehrig hit his third, a blow "that landed on the roof of a home on 20th Street and bounced on and on." It was a harbinger of things to come for the Yankee Iron Horse. Gehrig's superlative career would never escape Ruth's gargantuan shadow.

Lou Gehrig . . . he was the guy who hit all those homers the year Ruth set the record.

Franklin P. Adams

I'm not a headline guy, and we might as well face it. I'm just a guy who's in the there every day. The fellow who follows the Babe in the batting order. When Babe's turn at bat is over, whether he strikes out or belts a home run, the fans are still talking about him when I come up. If I stood on my head at the plate, nobody'd pay any attention.

Lou Gehrig

Miller Huggins had more nicknames than most guys in baseball did: "Little Mr. Everywhere," "Mighty Mite," and "Rabbit," because he was tiny, wiry, and fast. "The Lawyer" because he studied law before baseball, and "Hug" just because.

Jay David

Waite Hoyt's pitching has been a treat— a treat for those who can see something other than murdering the ball. Such control, such transition from one speed to another, such art in the pleasure of his slow curve. There isn't a better right-handed pitcher in all baseball than Hoyt as he is at present. He is the refinement of skill.

New York Herald Tribune

He made you feel like a giant.

Mark Koenig
on manager Miller Huggins

Was Bill Dickey the greatest catcher the game has ever known? Connie Mack thought so, as did Ed Barrow and Ty Cobb.

**William Hageman and
Warren Wilbert**

He was a precisely controlled dynamo of fury: bat cocked high, feet planted wide, perfectly still until the final moment, when he advanced his left foot a mere inch or two and turned loose one of baseball's thunderbolt swings.

Donald Honig
on Joe DiMaggio

He is splendid in his line of work and we need him in there.

Casey Stengel
*on Joe DiMaggio, when asked on
the day-to-day status of the injured
Yankee Clipper in late June 1949*

Now wait a minute, you're going into too big a man. Maybe he woulda been an astronaut if he wanted. He could hit some balls off the moon and see if they'd carry. There were a lot of great ones and Ruth could pitch, too, but this fella is the best I ever had.

Casey Stengel
on Joe DiMaggio

When Joe came into the clubhouse it was like a senator or a president coming in.

Billy Martin
*as a Yankee rookie in 1950,
on the regal presence of
teammate Joe DiMaggio*

When he walked into the clubhouse, the lights flickered. Joe DiMaggio was a star.

Pete Sheehy
*long-time Yankees
clubhouse custodian*

The best base runner I ever saw.

Joe McCarthy
*manager (1931–46),
on Joe DiMaggio*

There's so much ground out there in Yankee Stadium, the toughest center field in baseball. Only the great ones can play it. And he did it so easily. You never saw him make a great catch. You never saw him dive for a ball. He didn't have to. He was already there to catch it.

Joe McCarthy
on Joe DiMaggio

The best thing he had—and I'll give you a tip—was his head.

Casey Stengel
on the Yankee Clipper

You couldn't chip that bat. That's the way DiMaggio's wood was on the bats. He would ask for that type of wood. Being an old fisherman, he knew about the trees.

Phil Rizzuto
from O Holy Cow!

I would like to take the great DiMaggio fishing. They say his father was a fisherman.

Ernest Hemingway
The Old Man and the Sea

Mickey Mantle. Outside of Babe Ruth, it was probably the best baseball name ever invented. His father picked the name, in honor of Mickey Cochrane, a Hall of Fame catcher for Detroit.

Mickey Herskowitz
author and sportswriter

What can you say after you have said how great he was?

Gene Woodling
*outfielder (1949–54),
on Mickey Mantle*

Mantle was the last in a line of almost mythical New York Yankee sluggers who rose above their numbers and beyond the Hall of Fame: Babe Ruth, Lou Gehrig, Joe DiMaggio. He may have been the last true star who was not identified by the money he made.

Mickey Herskowitz

His fame, his legend, his popularity, seemed to rest not so much on what he achieved—and that was considerable— but on what he promised: a thrill with every at bat, power, speed, and the poetry of youth. . . . He played the game the way little kids did in their dreams.

Mickey Herskowitz
on Mickey Mantle

When I was 20 years old, I was a better ballplayer than [I was in my prime]. I could hit better, run faster, and throw better. Yet they farmed me out to the minor leagues. I was too young to take all the pressures of major league ball. When a boy of 20 can handle it, you've got yourself a real special ballplayer—a Williams, a Musial, or a Cobb.

Mickey Mantle, 1961

No man in the history of baseball had as much power as Mickey Mantle. No man. You're not talking about ordinary power. Dave Kingman had power. Willie Mays had power. Then when you're talking about Mantle—it's an altogether different level.

Billy Martin
second baseman
(1950–53, '55–57),
and five-time Yankee manager

You'll never be a ballplayer. Take my advice, son, and forget baseball. Get into some other line of business.

Branch Rickey
to Yogi Berra, after Berra's unsuccessful tryout with the St. Louis Cardinals

In recent years there has been a tendency to rate Yogi Berra as the second-best hitting catcher of the modern era—behind Johnny Bench. I have always found this comparison puzzling. Berra leads Bench in batting average by nearly 20 points as well as in RBIs and total runs scored, despite the fact that Yogi had fewer at-bats. Bench leads only in total home runs and ties Berra for total fielding average.

Phil Rizzuto

No one *feels* baseball better than Yogi Berra, no one relishes the excitement of its competition more, no one reacts more quickly to its constant challenge. He is a masterpiece of a ballplayer.

Robert W. Creamer

He was a teacher and there wasn't a guy on any Casey Stengel team who wasn't a better player for having played under him.

Tony Cuccinello
15-year major league infielder
(1930–45)

I played for Casey Stengel before and after he was a genius.

Warren Spahn
Hall of Fame pitcher who was sent to the minors by Stengel when both were with the Boston Braves in 1942. Spahn hooked up again with the Old Professor twenty-three years later as a New York Met

He was a brilliant strategist and could play the press the way Heifetz played the fiddle.

Maury Allen
on Casey Stengel

I give the man a point for speed. I do this because Maris can run fast. Then I give him a point because he can slide fast. I give him another point because he can bunt. I also give him a point because he can field. He is very good around the fences—sometimes on top of the fences. Next, I give him a point because he can throw. A right fielder has to be a thrower or he's not a right fielder. So I add up my points, and I've got five for him before I even come to his hitting. I would say this is a good man.

Casey Stengel

Reggie Jackson is a lot like Mantle. They think a 380-foot homer doesn't count. They both tried to hit the ball 500 feet.

Joe DiMaggio

He's the only guy in baseball who can carry a club for a month. And the hell with what you hear. He hustles every minute on the field.

Thurman Munson
catcher (1969–79), on Reggie Jackson, before the free agent slugger signed with New York

Ron Guidry's the most impressive pitcher I've ever seen. He's more impressive than [Tom] Seaver or [Jim] Palmer or [Nolan] Ryan.

Sparky Lyle
pitcher (1972–78)

His greatest asset is not his bat. It is his incredible ability to get rid of the ball. It sometimes seems that he throws it before he has caught it.

Newsday
on Thurman Munson during his rookie season. The Yankee catcher batted .302 and was named AL Rookie of the Year

He thought his job with the Yankees consisted of this one important thing: playing baseball hard, all the time. Walk up to the plate when the pain in the knees was like daggers. Make the throw to second base when the right arm was aching and useless. Run the bases like a fullback when one more collision might take him out for good.

Mike Lupica
New York Daily News, eulogizing Thurman Munson

SHRINE TO NO. 7

Mantle once said that every time he swung the bat, he was swinging for a home run.

Lonnie Wheeler

SO MUCH enters into the making of the myth of Mickey Mantle. His 534 career home runs elevated him to an exclusive sluggers' club. There was the always tantalizing "what if?" about his injury-plagued career, which never ceased to ask what he could have done on two good legs. Being a switch-hitter generated fabled overtones as well. The boyish good looks, shyness, and sonorous alliterative name also figured into the equation of the Commerce Comet as an American icon.

But likely the largest single factor contributing to his immense status was the Superman quality of the tape-measure home runs. Heroic deeds had found a new definition.

> Prodigious shots of sheer raw power,
> Past Griffith's and Briggs' light towers.
>
> from "Mantle Days,"
> *Echoes from the Ball Park*

They say no one ever ripped the ball like Mickey Mantle. Even Ruth, who awed crowds with his shocking displays of power couldn't match The Mick for combustive explosion at the moment of impact.

Mantle first staggered baseball followers with his monumental blast off the Washington Senators' Chuck Stobbs in 1953 at Griffith Stadium, one of Mantle's favorite hitting grounds. Lonnie Wheeler penned a fabulous description of this enormous moment (pages 106–7). He states that the term "tape-measure home run" was born at that instant.

The tale of the tape continued unabated in Mantle's triple crown year of 1956, when, on opening day, he belted his first at-bat of the season and another in the sixth inning clear out of Griffith Stadium again.

In the first game of a Memorial Day double-header that same year against Washington, at Yankee Stadium, where no fair ball had ever been hit out, Mantle walloped a Pedro Ramos pitch that slammed into the famed facade 117 feet above field level and over the 370-foot sign. It came within 18 inches of escaping the stadium. Estimates say the ball would have traveled between 550 and 600 feet. Several years later, Mantle again hit the right-field facade, on May 22, 1963, barely missing an out-of-the-park homer by inches, this time off Kansas City's Bill Fischer.

Detroit's Briggs Stadium was another favorite Mantle target. In the course of his career, he hit four balls over the roof—the only player ever to accomplish that feat. On June 18, 1956, The Mick towered a shot off the Tigers' Paul Foytack that soared over the right-field roof, which stands 110-feet high, directly over the 370-foot sign. The ball landed on Trumbull Avenue, where a man listening to the game on a radio outside the park retrieved the ball, returning the following day to have Mantle sign it.

On the afternoon the Yankees clinched their fifth American League pennant in six years—September 18, 1956—Mantle clocked one over the left-center field roof in Chicago.

"It was the longest ball ever hit at Comiskey Park," said Mantle. "They measured it at 550 feet. Now that the Sox have played their last game there, that's one record I can be sure will never be surpassed."

[It is] one of baseball's landmark home runs. . . . If it has kinship in baseball history, it is with Ruth's "called shot" in the 1932 World Series; but where Ruth's clout crowned a legend, Mantle's was the launching of one. Of all the fabled home runs in baseball history, Mantle's alone stands for something other than dramatic victory. This particular cannon shot stands for might and power; it is its own colossal symbol.

Donald Honig
historian and author, on Mantle's 565-foot home run, April 17, 1953, Griffith Stadium, Washington, D.C.

He came so close to making history that he made it.

Robert W. Creamer
historian and author, on Mantle's shot that nearly cleared the right-field facade of Yankee Stadium, May 30, 1956

Just a day or two after Mickey Elvin Mantle [was born], his dad hit an incredible blast at Griffith Stadium in Washington, D.C. It was on this occasion that the term "tape-measure home run" was coined. Mantle, batting right-handed against Washington lefty Chuck Stobbs, hit a rising line drive that left the playing field at the 391-foot mark. It grazed the 60-foot beer sign on top of the football scoreboard behind the bleachers, carried across Fifth Street, and landed in a backyard on Oakdale Street. The Yankees' publicity director, Red Patterson, was so stunned that he felt he had to do something to verify Mantle's unbelievable drive. He immediately dashed out of the press box, left the stadium, and found the spot where witnesses said the ball had landed. Then he paced off the distance and fixed it at 565 feet. . . . Later the Senators marked the spot on the beer sign where the ball had left the park, but Washington manager Bucky Harris grew angry at it and demanded that the marker be removed. Though Mantle probably hit longer home runs, the 565-footer still stands as the longest hit ever measured.

Lonnie Wheeler

In May 1963, batting against Bill Fischer of the Kansas City Athletics, Mantle hit what may have been the longest home run ever. Earlier in the game, Mantle's knees had buckled as he faced a change-of-pace pitch from Fischer. The Kansas City bench had given the great slugger a hard time over that.

But in the bottom of the 11th inning, Mantle got another crack at the junkball artist. This time, Fischer tried to slip a fastball by the Mick, and Mantle connected with all of his might. He said that it was the only time in his life that he actually saw the bat bend in his hands when he made contact with the ball. It was a bigger bat than players use today, and it sent Fischer's pitch on an incredible high, straight line toward the right-field roof at Yankee Stadium. By the accounts of those present, the ball was still rising when it struck the facade of the roof. One scientist has estimated the drive would have traveled a minimum of 620 feet. If it was still rising, as observers said, it would have gone much farther, possibly approaching 700 feet.

Lonnie Wheeler

Nobody's half as good as Mickey Mantle.

Al Kaline
Detroit Tigers legend and Hall of Famer, in reply to a fan who had taunted the Tiger great by saying he wasn't half as good as Mantle

MANTLE DAYS

There were few boys in '53,
Who didn't wish to be like Mickey.

Fervant youths without exception,
Mirrored the swing of number 7.

Scintillating smooth switch-hitter;
Followed the great Yankee Clipper.

Commerce Comet, swift as a breeze,
Basepaths ablaze on horrible knees.

Mate of Berra, Ford and Skowron,
Woodling, Bauer and Billy Martin.

Bronx Bombers, M&M boys,
The Stadium's rapturous, thunderous noise.

Prodigious shots of sheer raw power,
Past Griffith's and Briggs' light towers.

A deep-bleacher Ballantine blast,
Mel Allen cries, "How 'bout that!"

Legend from a dynasty,
Three-time AL MVP.

'56 triple-crown king,
Seven gold World Series rings.

One of Gotham's Mighty Three:
Duke, The Mick, Say-Hey Willie.

Eighth all-time: career home runs,
Fifty-four in '61.

Ev'ry card collector's ambition:
His '52 Topps in mint condition.

But heroes held too high on shoulders,
Often fall when it's all over.

His final words came truthfully:
"Listen, kids, don't be like me."

We'll not likely soon see his likes,
This classic Yankee in pinstripes.

Alan Ross

THE VELVETEEN
MICKEY MANTLE

Once upon at time, a little boy with baseball in his eyes happily spread his 1952 and 1953 New York Yankee player cards on the floor in front of him. Usually he had enough cards from the same team to neatly arrange in the shape of a baseball diamond, filling all nine positions.

The Chicago White Sox, visitors this day, were out in the field. Cardboard likenesses of Chico Carrasquel, Nellie Fox, and pitcher Billy Pierce fairly trembled, awaiting the terrifying sluggers onslaught from the Bronx: Mantle, Berra, Bauer, Collins, Woodling.

The boy positioned the Mantle card, his favorite, in the batter's box. Holding a pencil in his right hand (Mickey would be batting right-handed today against the Sox's southpaw ace) and rolling a small piece of tin foil between the fingers of his left hand, the kid let sail the miniature ball toward The Mick. With a mighty swing of his Empire No. 2 "Louisville Slugger," Mantle arched the little spheroid over the living room couch for a three-run Ballantine blast, Rizzuto and Martin crossing the plate in front of him.

I love my '53 Mickey Mantle. And my '51 Vic Raschi. I'm still emotionally connected to my '52 Johnny Mize and the '55 Bowman Gil McDougald on the color TV screen. From the years 1951 to 1957, I collected baseball and football cards. Most of those youthful treasures survived unscathed. These relics that stare back at me from an old cardboard box are the vaunted heroes of my past.

It should be enough to merely revere them for what they are, but in the ensuing years a foreboding, incessant presence has been felt with increasing force—*collectibles*.

Like carpetbaggers invading the land of innocence, trading card dealers now hold reign and dominion over an empire that has turned ruddy-cheeked boys into opportunistic businessmen. Today a young card fan is a cool-headed investor first, and a collector second. Back in 1952, you never heard the qualifying phrases *mint, near mint, excellent, very good,* etc. So I thought I'd set up my own evaluation rules.

They are based upon Margery Williams' wonderful children's classic, *The Velveteen Rabbit*. In the story, a child's beloved stuffed animal (rabbit) is earmarked by the parents for extinction, its fate largely determined by its increasingly shabby appearance. The ragamuffin rabbit creates the perception that some of his worth has been lost over the years. The rabbit's owner, a little boy, shows greater wisdom, knowing you don't toss something of value just because it's old and decrepit. The once-velveteen rabbit became bald because the little boy had loved all its hair off!

Now cut to the old, decrepit baseball cards—the Fords, Skowrons, Berras, et al. I can only guess that the diagonal crease in my '53 Mickey Mantle or the dog-eared corners of my '51 Vic Raschi got that way because I loved them in a fashion similar to the child's love for his velveteen rabbit. With great excitement I would slide the card-of-the-day into my lunch box or—worse from *Beckett*'s standpoint—into my back pocket, and head out to meet the school bus.

I don't want any passionless dealer handling my velveteen Mantle. Give me a man who will look upon a '52 Topps Bob Feller—marked by just the waning hint of rubber band indentation on the sides—and smile, knowing Rapid Robert and his Cleveland teammates were probably scattered on some living room rug countless times in fantasy struggles against the fearsome Yanks. In that regard, maybe I could make a case for

AUTHOR'S COLLECTION

charging even *more* for bent or creased cards, the inference being that a card that has had its hair loved off would have inestimable value.

It's a wonder these little pieces of colored cardboard survived the fervid passions of youth. But there is a happy ending. The velveteen Mickey Mantle is *still* alive and well today.

8

GREAT MOMENTS

What if Martin don't catch Rob-A-Son's fly ball, which he did splendidly.

Casey Stengel

on Billy Martin's dashing game-and series-saving infield catch of Jackie Robinson's bases-loaded pop-up in the seventh inning of Game 7 of the 1952 World Series to preserve a 4-2 New York victory over Brooklyn

IT WOULD take several libraries and most of the room at the National Archives to hold all the landmark moments that have filled the pages of New York Yankees annals.

From the days of the Highlanders and Jack Chesbro's 41-victory season in 1904 to the Babe's called shot in the 1932 World Series, to Gehrig's four homers against the Athletics that same year, to the famous passed-ball error of the Dodgers' Mickey Owen in the '41 Series that enabled Tommy Henrich to reach first safely and keep a winning Yank drive alive, to Don Larsen's perfect game in '56, the same year as Mantle's triple crown, to Roger Maris's 61 home runs in '61, to Reggie Jackson's homer clinic in the '77 Series, to Bucky Dent's KO home run against the Red Sox in the '78 AL playoff game, to the perfecto games of David Wells and David Cone in '98 and '99 respectively, to the incredible world championship run of the late-twentieth-century Bronx Bombers, the Yankees have been involved in more immortal moments than the rest of baseball combined.

Savor a handful of history, New York Yankees style.

Thirty thousand gasped, according to the press. Its length was not determined—the tape measure, like air-conditioning, awaited invention—but this one, to center field, was so extravagant that Cleveland catcher Joe Sewell demanded the umpires check Ruth's bat, arguing that no mortal could hit a ball that far without the aid of lead in the weapon. The umpires dutifully went over the bludgeon and concluded what all the world knew. It wasn't the bat. It was Ruth.

John Mosedale
on what was regarded as the second longest home run ever hit by Babe Ruth, in a 6-4 victory over Cleveland in June 1927

The Babe made his triumphant, almost regal tour of the bases. He jogged around slowly, touched each base firmly, and when he embedded his spikes in the rubber disk to record officially Homer 60, hats were tossed in the air, papers were torn up and tossed crazily, and the spirit of celebration permeated the place.

The New York Times
October 1, 1927

They could no more have stopped Babe Ruth from hitting that home run that gave him a new world record than you could have stopped a locomotive by sticking your foot in front of it. Once he had that 59, that Number 60 was as sure as the rising sun. A more determined athlete than George Herman Ruth never lived.

Paul Gallico
New York Daily News,
October 1, 1927

The Babe was a boisterous, big-hearted child of nature who exuded color out of every pore. He was a legend come to life. Paul Bunyan in the flesh. . . . No one but Babe would have dared to point to the bleachers where he would then hit a home run off Charlie Root in the 1932 World Series.

Arthur Daley
The New York Times

I didn't exactly point to any spot. All I wanted to do was give the thing a ride out of the park. I used to pop off a lot about hitting homers.

Babe Ruth
to Chicago sportswriter John Carmichael, about his famous "called-shot" home run off the Chicago Cubs' Charlie Root in the 1932 World Series

It was the second four-game sweep in [World] Series history, the only other being the Braves' triumph over the 1914 Athletics. . . . In 1932 and in 1938 the Yankees swept the Cubs; in 1939, the Reds; and in 1950, the Phillies. Those were sweeps. There were six other Yankee world championships between 1927 and 1950.

John Mosedale
referring to New York's sweep of
Pittsburgh in the 1927 World Series

It took the two most expensive aspirins in history.

Wally Pipp
first baseman (1915–25)

Pipp made the fateful choice to sit out a game due to a headache on June 1, 1925, and was replaced by a youngster named Lou Gehrig. The Iron Horse went on to play in 2,130 consecutive games; Pipp never made it back into the New York lineup.

He will think about it every day for the rest of his life, just like I do.

Don Larsen
*who pitched the only perfect game
in World Series history, on David
Wells's perfect game in 1998*

My top memory was Don Larsen's perfect game in 1956. Next, of course, was Reggie [Jackson]'s three homers in the final game of 1977.

Bob Sheppard
*New York's incomparable public
address announcer since 1951*

I can remember it clear as a bell. "Pinch-hitting, No. 8, Dale Mitchell." At that moment, my mother put her arm around me and said, "Don't tell anyone this is your dad, 'cause if he gets a hit, these fans might kill us." That made me realize that this was something important.

Bo Mitchell
*whose father, Dale, was the last
out in Don Larsen's perfect game
in the 1956 World Series*

What if the ball don't hit him in the throat, dontcha think we win it and I'm out with a championship even though I'm discharged?

Casey Stengel

In the eighth inning, a ground ball bounced up and hit shortstop Tony Kubek in the throat during Game 7 of the 1960 World Series. The Pirates scored five runs in that inning to take a two-run lead into the ninth. The Yankees managed to get two in the top half to tie it, but this Series will always be remembered for Bill Mazeroski's bottom-of-the-ninth World Series–winning home run. It would be the last game Stengel managed for the Yankees after recording ten pennants and seven world championships in his twelve years at the New York helm.

The essential difference between Ruth and Maris was not merely that Maris was a better all-around ball player, but that Maris had to worry about Ruth and Ruth didn't have to worry about Maris. The Babe swung with a free mind, and, as I remember it, often with an empty mind. The difference wasn't that Maris had a livelier ball or bat than Ruth had but that he had a livelier imagination—and that is no advantage to a ball player practicing his profession under savage pressure in a howling stadium.

James Reston
The New York Times

Maris was never treated as a champion because he challenged the immortals and won.

Mickey Mantle

I know how we older players and you veteran writers feel about the records. I happen to hold one myself, the 56-game batting streak. . . . But that will go, the home run record will go. The effort of some people, half of them biased, the other half old-timers who think baseball died with Matty and Johnson, to give the impression that the game has made no progress is stupid.

Joe DiMaggio
during Roger Maris's race to eclipse Ruth's home run record in 1961

One guy wrote that I don't deserve to break Ruth's record. Now I admire Ruth. He was the greatest. But what am I supposed to do, stop hitting homers? They make it sound as if I'd be committing a sin if I broke the record.

Roger Maris

I saw it was a good fastball. I was ready and I connected. As soon as I hit it, I knew it was number 61; it was the only time that the number of the homer ever flashed into my mind as I hit it. Then I heard the tremendous roar of the crowd. I could see them all standing. Then my mind went blank.

Roger Maris

I knew he hit the stuff out of it, but I didn't think it was going to be a home run. I turned around and then saw the thing going way up. I give Roger all the credit in the world. I gave him what I feel was my best fastball and he hit it.

Tracy Stallard
Boston Red Sox pitcher of record on Maris's 61st home run

Whether I beat Ruth's record or not is for others to say. But it gives me a wonderful feeling to know that I'm the only man in history to hit 61 home runs. Nobody can take that away from me. Babe Ruth was a big man in baseball, maybe the biggest ever. I'm not saying I am of his caliber, but I'm glad to say I hit more than he did in a season.

Roger Maris

Commissioner Ford Frick attached an asterisk next to the 61 homers in the record book because Roger Maris failed to hit them in the first 154 games, which happened to be the schedule when Ruth got the 60. I thought it was a ridiculous ruling. It made no sense at all. Check further and you'll note that the same year, 1961, Sandy Koufax broke Christy Mathewson's National League strikeout record. Mathewson set it in 1903, when they played a 140-game schedule. But you won't find an asterisk attached to Koufax.

Mickey Mantle

That was one of the greatest exhibitions of playing third base I've seen in all my career.

Tommy Lasorda
Los Angeles Dodgers manager,
on Graig Nettles's outstanding
performance in Game 3 of the
1978 World Series

It is estimated that Nettles saved five runs on his diving, twisting stops of blistering smashes in the third, fifth, and sixth innings—twice when the bases were loaded.

I really didn't know whether it went over the wall or not.

Jeffrey Meier

Twelve-year-old Meier commented on his in-the-field-of-play catch of Derek Jeter's eighth-inning fly ball to right in the opening game of the 1996 American League Championship Series against the Baltimore Orioles. Umpire Rich Garcia ruled the shot a game-tying home run. The Yanks went on to win it 5-4 in the eleventh on a home run by Bernie Williams.

Me and the kid almost touched gloves. It was a routine fly ball. In my mind, there is no way in the world I would have dropped it. Merlin must have been in the air.

> **Tony Tarasco**
> *Baltimore Orioles right fielder,*
> *on the infamous catch by Yankees'*
> *"angel in the outfield" Jeffrey Meier*

Where's Jeffrey Meier when you need him?

> **Todd Zeile**
> *New York Mets first baseman*

Zeile's two-out sixth-inning shot with a runner on base came within an inch of clearing the left-field fence in Game 1 of the 2000 World Series at Yankee Stadium. The Yankees took the critical game, 4-3, in twelve innings.

My last comment to him leaving the bullpen was, "Don't just throw because your stuff is good. Concentrate on your pitches, because your stuff is so outstanding."

Mel Stottlemyre
to David Wells, just prior to his 4-0 perfect-game win against the Minnesota Twins, May 17, 1998

I think it's time for you to break out your knuckleball.

David Cone
to David Wells as the lefthander took the mound for the eighth inning of his perfect game.

The comment cracked up Wells. Later he credited Cone's remark as a key to helping him stay loose for the tension-packed last two innings.

To pitch a perfect game wearing pinstripes at Yankee Stadium, it's unbelievable.

David Wells

Big moments do have a way of following me around.

David Cone

It is the happiest day of my life. The way I did this is unbelievable. I don't know how to explain it. Today, they gave me a chance to come through. . . . It's a dream come true.

Luis Sojo
infielder (1998–), on his World Series–winning hit up the middle that gave the Yankees their twenty-sixth world championship

The biggest game I ever pitched was
when I jumped on a raft and left Cuba.

Orlando Hernández

9

THE GREAT YANKEE TEAMS

The defeat in the 1926 World Series was a dark interlude between the Yankees' unexpected triumph in the pennant race that year and their rise in 1927 to a peak which many believe they have never surpassed. This, they say, was the team. Greater than any that had gone before, greater than any that has followed.

Frank Graham

THE LEGENDARY little man, Yankees manager Miller Huggins, once said: "A team is like a bridge hand. You've got to get up your strongest suit."

A pinstripe suit at that.

It's safe to say the Yanks have won their share of bridge hands over the years. They've also crossed a few bridges when they've had to in order to claim whatever prize lay ahead, for no team in professional sports history has ever strung together so many championship titles: thirty-seven American League flags and twenty-six World Series crowns.

That'll buy you a bunch of bridges.

Who was the best? The 1927 Murderers' Row team, the DiMaggio-led Bombers of 1939, the '61 powerhouse led by the M&M boys, the Reggie Jackson–led Yanks of '77, or the end-of-the-century New Yorkers who took four championships in five years?

Yankee fans, players, personnel, and opponents likely won't ever find agreement on that one.

Since the Yankees took off like one of Ruth's home runs, neither failing nor falling, there was a shortage of big, in the sense of significant, games. The Yankees roared off on opening day and never looked back, never fell from first place. This can be regarded as dull or seen as something marvelous to behold, like a [Franklin D.] Roosevelt presidential campaign, or Joe Louis touching someone up, or the Marx Brothers.

John Mosedale
on the 1927 Yankees

I know of no one who could have taken over a bunch of artificial prima donnas such as was handed to Miller Huggins when he first came to New York and turned them ultimately into a perfect, machine-like organism.

Joe Williams
New York World Telegram

Ruth the greatest ballplayer who ever lived. Combs, a star of the first magnitude. Meusel, the greatest thrower who ever lived. The three of them and Lazzeri each knocked in 100 runs that year. Gehrig, a superstar, one of the greatest. Lazzeri, a star, a great thrower, good hitter. Koenig, erratic but he made it up with his hitting. Dugan. Ah, one of the lesser lights, but yes, I'll go for this: I could field as well as anybody in those days. The catching, ordinary. Hoyt, a star. Pennock, a star. Pipgras, a good pitcher. Moore, the best relief pitcher I ever saw.

Joe Dugan
on the '27 Yankees

They don't just beat you, they break your heart.

Joe Judge
*Washington Senators first
baseman (1915–32),
on the 1927 Yankees*

If Lou and Babe take a couple of days off, the pitchers turn in unbelievable performances.

Fred Lieb
*on the 1927 Yanks hurlers, who
led the majors in complete games
with 45, 40 of them victories*

Writers who saw the 1927 team know that subsequent years have not seen its equal.

Dan Daniel

History, like life, is unfair, and the 1927 team is remembered for scoring the most runs, not for giving up the fewest.

John Mosedale

I certainly have no desire to say anything about the pitchers of 1927, but I believe that the hurlers of today are throwing more varieties than the 1927 gang did.

Joe DiMaggio
1961

The 1927 Yankees probably beat themselves less than any ball club that ever lived.

Waite Hoyt

In the 1939 Series, [Joe] McCarthy's Yanks clobbered the Reds 4-0 to win an unprecedented fourth straight World Championship. . . . Not [John] McGraw's Giants, not Connie Mack's A's, not even [Miller] Huggins's Yankees—no one had ever accomplished that feat.

John Tullius

We'd hit the home run, yes, but it was a team of players that played the game right and knew how to play it.

Tony Kubek
on the 1961 Yankees

You look at that lineup, from top to bottom, and a guy like Johnny Blanchard sitting on the bench? God, you know they're tough.

Warren Hacker
twelve-year major league
pitcher, on the '61 Yanks

We're the best team money can't buy, and they're the best team money can buy. They have a lot of players who play their best under pressure.

George Brett
Kansas City Royals Hall of
Famer, on the 1978 Yankees

There wasn't a Murderers' Row; there was no Bambino. It was all about being a team.

Jay David
*on the 1996 world champion
New York Yankees*

They're not intimidating. It's not like they're sending up Murderers' Row, but they get hits when they have to get hits.

Bobby Valentine
on the 1998 Yankees

I never saw the '27 Yankees or the '39 Yankees, but I did see the Oakland A's of the early '70s and Cincinnati's Big Red Machine, and this is the best team I've ever seen.

Joe Torre
on the record-setting 1998 Yanks

We don't have one big guy. We have a team full of big guys.

Tim Raines
outfielder–designated hitter,
on the 1998 world champions

You don't win 114 games by being lucky.

Mike Hargrove
manager, Cleveland Indians,
on the 1998 Bombers

I think we can hold up to one of those great teams because of what we have accomplished. I think our run of five postseasons is pretty damn good. With free agency and players changing teams so often, to be able to find ourselves here again is a pretty good run. I think our ballclub should be right up there with any of the clubs that have put something together.

Joe Torre
on his 2000 world champions

I will say this, I don't know if any other team in New York has ever done any better.

George Steinbrenner
on the 2000 New York Yankees

They may say it's the greatest team ever, but you'll get arguments from the great Yankee teams—the '27 Yankees, the Yankee teams that won five World Series in a row (1949–53). But absolutely, I think you have an argument for this being the greatest team.

Reggie Jackson
on the 2000 Yanks

We may not have the best players, but we certainly have the best team.

Joe Torre
on the 2000 Bronx Bombers

What I probably most admire and am most proud of with this team is their resolve and grittiness.

Joe Torre
on the 2000 club

This team never will be confused with the great pinstripers of past lore, the ballclubs of Ruth, Gehrig, DiMaggio or Mantle. But it will be remembered as a group of low-key pros led by their redoubtable manager.

Jon Saraceno
USA Today, on the 2000 Yanks

This is a group of 25 MVPs. Every game there is a new hero.

Derek Jeter
2000 World Series MVP

They seem like they just pound on you. You don't get a reprieve even with the number six, seven, eight, or nine hitters. Normally, you get an out or two down there.

Al Leiter
New York Mets pitcher,
on the bottom half of the 2000
New York Yankees lineup

These guys had a team concept that was tremendous. I've had better teams, but none with a bigger heart.

George Steinbrenner
on the 2000 world champions

They knew how to do it because they've done it before. They told themselves they're a great team—and believed it. They knew the map, the road they had to follow. . . . Put the emphasis on team. This is one of the all-time great baseball teams. If you talk about great individuals and superstars, this team doesn't finish high.

Reggie Jackson
on the 2000 Yanks

The mark of a team isn't winning the championship; it's how you defend the championship.

George Steinbrenner

Babe Ruth made a grave mistake when he gave up pitching. Working once a week, he might have lasted a long time and become a great star.

Tris Speaker
spring 1921—the year Ruth clouted 59 home runs

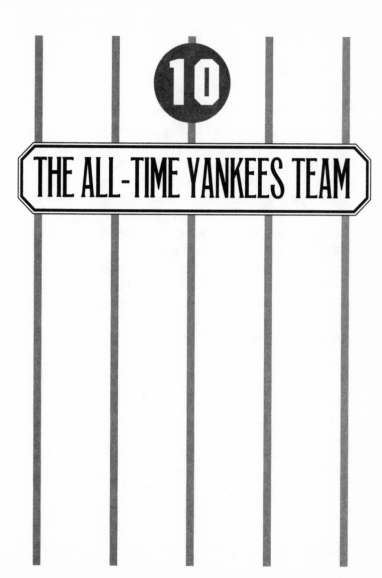

10

THE ALL-TIME YANKEES TEAM

PICK AN all-time New York Yankees team?

Absolutely—with the courage of Karl Wallenda, the insolence of Don Rickles, and the resolve of a marine.

Naturally, we'll offend some—maybe many. But there'll be none of that pussy-footing "move Mantle to right to make room for DiMag in center" low-rent cowardice here. With the nerve of a demolitions expert, it's one person per position—no second-place consolations. And forget about that messy designated hitter business, too.

Envision the classic tones of Yankees public-address legend Bob Sheppard announcing this lineup in the cavernous reverberation of the old Yankee Stadium.

"Your attention, please, ladies and gentlemen—now batting for the Yankees . . ."

Lou Gehrig, *first base*
Tony Lazzeri, *second base*
Graig Nettles, *third base*
Phil Rizzuto, *shortstop*
Yogi Berra, *catcher*
Bob Meusel, *left field*
Joe DiMaggio, *center field*
Babe Ruth, *right field*
Whitey Ford, *left-handed pitcher*
Red Ruffing, *right-handed pitcher*
Casey Stengel, *manager*

Kid, that was the greatest I ever seen.

Babe Ruth
*to Lou Gehrig, June 3, 1932, after
Gehrig slammed four consecutive
home runs against the Philadelphia
Athletics—a feat Ruth himself never
achieved—and was robbed of a fifth
on a great catch by Al Simmons*

LOU GEHRIG

FIRST BASE

Believe me it's painful to ask Moose Skowron and the great Yankee captain Don Mattingly, an American League MVP and nine-time Gold Glove winner, to take a seat. But when you're stocked with legends, the average superstar sits.

It's hard to imagine anyone doing anything spectacularly enough to oust Lou Gehrig from his rightful spot on any all-time Yankees team.

The famed Iron Horse wrote the book on endurance until a precocious Baltimore shortstop added an additional chapter in 1995.

The two-time American League MVP's true legacy with the Yankees rests in the incredible fact that he was so steady and productive while continually being overshadowed by Babe Ruth and, in the later stages of his career, by a young Joe DiMaggio. Yet, as was his way, Lou simply did it. Every day. Quietly.

Franklin P. Adams summed it up when he said, "[Gehrig] was the guy who hit all those homers the year Ruth set the record."

That young Eyetalian is a ball player. When things get tough over there, the others don't look to Ruth or any of the other veterans. They look to Lazzeri.

Timmy Connelly
American League umpire, one month after Tony Lazzeri joined the Yankees in 1926

TONY LAZZERI

SECOND BASE

The keystone kingpin of Murderers' Row, Tony Lazzeri was a hugely popular Italian-American who came to the Yankees in 1926 after a spectacular minor league season at Salt Lake City, where he hit 60 homers and drove in 222 runs.

"Poosh 'Em Up" Tony's leadership presence was an immediate factor in the success of the legendary 1927 club, as noted by American League umpire Timmy Connelly.

Lazzeri is still an all-time leader in many career categories, ranking in the Yankees' top eleven all-time in runs, hits, doubles, triples, and RBIs.

He is part of one of the greatest moments in baseball history—the bases-loaded strikeout victim of thirty-nine-year-old Grover Cleveland Alexander in the seventh inning of the seventh game of the 1926 World Series against the Cardinals. Alexander hung a one-strike pitch, which Lazzeri hammered just inches foul of a home run, and then fooled him with a low-and-away breaking ball that killed the Yankees' rally, giving the title to St. Louis.

In the 1937 World Series, Lazzeri's last season with New York, he batted .400 against the New York Giants. The Yanks won it in five games.

Graig Nettles' uncanny style is not merely his diving stops. Even more impressive is the way he instantly jumps back to his feet (no jack-in-the-box ever popped faster), whirls and throws unerringly to first or second. His sense of direction is unsurpassed.

Murray Chass
sportswriter and author

GRAIG NETTLES

THIRD BASE

Nettles's mix of bat and glove makes him a clear-cut choice at the Hot Corner. The eleven-year Yankee (1973–83) hit for power, ranking only behind Hall of Fame legends Ruth, Mantle, Gehrig, DiMaggio, and Berra in career home runs (250). Nettles's ability to hit with men on base also earned him a spot in the Yankees all-time top ten list in RBIs, too.

The two-time Gold Glove winner's sterling play in the field drew oohs and ahhs from teammates, opponents, and fans alike, most notably his unbelievable series of stops during the third game of the 1978 World Series against the Los Angeles Dodgers. Nettles saved approximately five runs from being scored on diving, miraculous stabs of blistering smashes down the third-base line in the third, fifth, and sixth innings—twice when the bases were loaded.

"You ought to see some of the balls hit down to him," once enthused ace reliever and former Cy Young Award winner Sparky Lyle. "He dives, makes unbelievable plays, half in defense of his life, half just in defense."

Ty Cobb once said that only two players, Phil Rizzuto and Stan Musial, would have been stars in Cobb's time. He included Rizzuto's exceptional ability to hit to any field, and to lay down a bunt where it was most effective, plus his all-around defensive genius.

Jay David
author

PHIL RIZZUTO

SHORTSTOP

The Scooter made a splash in the spring training camp of 1941, the year after he was voted MVP of the minor league's American Association. In quick order, he replaced incumbent shortstop Frank Crosetti, then set out on a hall-of-fame career for the next eleven seasons, not counting three years out for military service.

It required no jury of peers to identify Phil Rizzuto as the class of the American League at short. His quick reactions, hustle, ability to hit to all fields, bunting skill, and, foremost, his talent for always making the right play quickly elevated him to a position of Yankee prominence. When the great DiMaggio was injured, it was to Rizzuto that the club turned for its inspiration and leadership, in essence to carry the team.

His all-around production in 1950 won him the league MVP award. The year before, he finished second in the MVP balloting, behind Ted Williams, when he led the Yankees in hits, runs, doubles, triples, stolen bases, and fewest errors by any American League shortstop.

And let's not forget the workout he gave the phrase "Holy Cow!" over the course of a lifetime.

Strange things happen to the reputations of players after they are retired. Yogi was always kind of a funny-looking little guy; he looked like if he was a piece of furniture you'd sand him off some. After he was retired, Joe Garagiola spent all those years telling funny stories about the kind of dopey stuff Yogi used to say and do. Gradually, the image of Yogi as a kind of short, knobby, comic-book reader grew larger and larger, and the memory of Yogi Berra as one hell of a catcher kind of drooped into the background.

Bill James
historian and author

YOGI BERRA

CATCHER

Yogi, as Bill James's comment implies, has become such an American icon of goofiness for his wonderful maxims featuring the best of malapropism, double meaning, and philosophical simplicity that the magnitude of his exceptional level of play during his eighteen years with the Bombers has faded into the background.

Almost forgotten is the fact that Berra was the Yankees dependable clutch hitter, batting cleanup through most of his career, from 1946 to 1963—the bedrock cornerstone of fourteen American League and ten World Series championship teams.

Berra also stands on the summit as a league MVP, claiming the prestigious honor three times. Nobody in the history of baseball has won more.

Hall of Famer Mel Ott, the former New York Giant who is a member of the exclusive five hundred home run club, once succinctly described the gifted Berra: "He stopped everything behind the plate and hit everything in front of it."

Forty years later [Waite] Hoyt wondered
why [Bob] Meusel was not in the Hall
of Fame. "He was as good a ballplayer
as I've ever seen," said the teammate
of Ruth and Gehrig, the foe of Cobb
and Speaker, the observer of Mays
and Mantle.

John Mosedale

BOB MEUSEL

LEFT FIELD

So much has been written about the prodigious throwing arm of Bob Meusel, the best in baseball during his time (1920–29), that his batting prowess is often overlooked.

Meusel was the fifth hitter in the fearsome Murderers' Row lineup the Yankees presented during the 1920s, meaning he batted immediately behind Ruth and Gehrig. He is the only Yankee slugger to lead the club in home runs other than Ruth during that hallowed decade, the heart of Ruth's prime, collecting 33 round-trippers in 1925 to lead the American League. His 138 RBIs that same year was tops, too. Meusel batted .311 lifetime with New York, good enough for sixth all-time in Yankee annals, and, as mentioned earlier, his gun was legendary.

He played the sun field—left field—at Yankee Stadium simply because Ruth couldn't. In fact, part of Meusel's assignment was to play the sun field in all ballparks where the Yanks played.

"Bob Meusel has one of the greatest arms in the business," Ruth once said. "I've seen him make a running catch in left then throw to first for a double play. That's real throwing."

Joe DiMaggio is the best all-around
player I've ever seen.

Mickey Mantle

JOE DIMAGGIO

CENTER FIELD

The magnificent Joe DiMaggio epitomizes the con-summate player performing with impeccable class, style, and grace.

The Yankee Clipper's entrance on the scene in the spring of 1936 came on the heels of Babe Ruth's exit. While New York looked to Lou Gehrig and Tony Lazzeri for inspiration, it would be the son of a San Francisco fisherman, who the previous year had hit safely in 61 straight games in the Pacific Coast League, who would become the main bombardier in the Bronx for the next thirteen seasons.

The toughest debate in baseball will continue to rage: Who was the best Yankee center fielder of all time, DiMaggio or Mantle? (I grew up with The Mick as my hero, so you can't cite favoritism here.) DiMaggio, like his fabled successor, was a three-time AL MVP. But what will always stand as a feat of iconic dimension is Joltin' Joe's immortal 56-game hitting streak in the summer of 1941.

Had Mantle remained healthy, the debate might not ever have been close.

Ruth won for baseball the number one
position in American sport. He did it
all with a large bat, a homely face, a
warming charm, a bad boy complex,
an inherent love for his fellow man,
an almost legendary indifference to
convention and a personal magnetism
more irresistible than the flute to
the cobra.

Waite Hoyt

BABE RUTH

RIGHT FIELD

He has become such a huge part of not only sports but American culture, it's sometimes hard to believe he was real.

But Ruth was no figment of the imagination. Known for his legendary power and gregarious character, he is undoubtedly the most popular sports figure of all time. His home run totals for single season and career were considered unreachable at one time, and ironically some people today continue to refer to the magic numbers of 60 and 714 with reverential awe, as if they were still the standard by which home runs are measured.

Forgotten in the hullabaloo over his prodigious hitting ability is the fact that Ruth was also one of the game's greatest pitchers, a man who held the World Series record for consecutive scoreless innings pitched for forty-three years.

You may wonder why Ruth earned only one MVP award (1923). Well, back then, previous winners were "retired" from future consideration.

The Bambino's larger-than-life personal appetites and legendary public image projected him into the nonpareil hero stratosphere.

Ruth is one man who actually lived up to it.

Whitey was a master. It was like watching a pitching textbook in the flesh.

Ralph Terry
pitcher (1956–57, '59–64),
on Whitey Ford

WHITEY FORD

LEFT-HANDED PITCHER

The "chairman of the board," as the flaxen-haired southpaw was known, was simply the best Yankees pitcher of all time. He remains, more than thirty years after his last pitch, the all-time Yankees leader in wins (236), strikeouts (1,956), and shutouts (45). In addition, he copped the American League's Cy Young Award in 1961.

Ford baffled batters with a dazzling array of off-speed pitches and pinpoint control. He was a money pitcher, too, holding World Series records for most wins (10) and most consecutive scoreless innings pitched (33⅓ innings), among others.

He was also an integral component of the famed Yankees' Rat Pack, along with good-time buddies Billy Martin and Mickey Mantle.

Ford's profound pitching awareness would often spellbind teammates. "Whitey was incredible," infielder Joe DeMaestri once said. "He not only knew where his pitch was going, he knew where the guy was going to hit it. He'd tell you to move a couple of steps to your left, and the guy would hit the ball right at you!"

Charley Ruffing, in more than five years in the Hub of the Universe, would lead the league in defeats, putting together a 39-96 record. Out of its boundless generosity, Boston then traded him to the Yankees, to become Red Ruffing of the Hall of Fame, four 20-game seasons in a row and a reputation as the hardest-hitting pitcher of his day.

John Mosedale

RED RUFFING

RIGHT-HANDED PITCHER

If you heard that a man's pitching record for his first five-plus seasons in the majors was a degrading 39-96, you'd likely say that he either lacked run support or he was just a run-of-the-mill hurler. If you then found out that he was in the Hall of Fame, you'd have to believe his enshrinement wasn't due to his pitching.

That's the unusual saga of all-time Yankees right-hander Red Ruffing, a bust in the 1920s but a supernova in the 1930s. Ruffing started his career with the Red Sox, where he toiled in misery until being traded to New York in 1930. Long story, short form: He went on to become the most prolific right-hander in Yankees history, winning 231 games in his fifteen seasons in the Bronx.

Four times in successive years (1936–39) Ruffing won more than twenty games a season, the only pitcher in Yankee annals to accomplish that feat.

To aid his own causes on the mound, Ruffing batted .269 lifetime, including stroking a phenomenal 36 homers and 273 RBIs. He is considered the best hitting pitcher in post-Ruthian baseball.

Keep your eyes off the scoreboard. Keep them on your own game. Pay attention to your own game.

Casey Stengel

CASEY STENGEL

MANAGER

Known as the "Old Perfesser," Casey Stengel was a bombastic Yankee mentor and field manager who was as irascible as he was lovable. Players tended to either adore him (Billy Martin) or dislike him (Phil Rizzuto). Regardless of others' affections or lack of them, Casey was a media-loving, nonstop lecturer and raconteur who had baseball running thick in his veins.

He was also the most successful major league manager in baseball history. Stengel stunned disbelievers and naysayers when he took the Yankee controls in 1949 and led the Bronx Bombers to five straight World Series crowns, a record that may stand forever. In all, Stengel was at the helm of ten American League championship teams and seven world champions while with New York.

Forgotten in the sea of Stengelese and popularity he enjoyed as a manager, particularly later on as the cartoony field boss of the New York Mets, was Stengel the ballplayer. He logged fourteen National League seasons as a fiery, hustling Pete Rose–type sparkplug with Brooklyn, Pittsburgh, Philadelphia, New York, and Boston.

RETIRED YANKEES NUMBERS

1 Billy Martin, *infielder* (1950–57)

3 Babe Ruth, *outfielder, pitcher* (1920–34)

4 Lou Gehrig, *infielder* (1923–39)

5 Joe DiMaggio, *outfielder* (1936–51)

7 Mickey Mantle, *outfielder* (1951–68)

8 Yogi Berra, *catcher* (1946–63)
   Bill Dickey, *catcher* (1928–46)

9 Roger Maris, *outfielder* (1960–66)

10 Phil Rizzuto, *shortstop* (1941–56)

15 Thurman Munson, *catcher* (1969–79)

16 Whitey Ford, *pitcher* (1950–67)

23 Don Mattingly, *outfielder* (1982–95)

32 Elston Howard, *outfielder, catcher* (1955–67)

37 Casey Stengel, *manager* (1949–60)

44 Reggie Jackson, *outfielder* (1977–81)

11

FIELDS OF PLAY

Colonel Ruppert's concrete cashbox.

A description of the new
Yankee Stadium in 1923

The old Hilltoppers' ball park was located on a north Manhattan hillside, at Broadway and 162nd St. My cousin and I went to [our] very first game in 1903. We sat in the bleachers. It rained and, due to inexperience, the front office hadn't provided for rain checks and made an announcement that anyone present could get in free the next day. Of course, everyone in New York turned up, claiming they'd been there when it rained, and there was a riot.

Dan Daniel

With a touch of *lèse majesté*, and perhaps avarice, the Giants allowed the American League club to share the Polo Grounds, beginning in 1913, by which time they were called the Yankees, a name given them by Jim Price, sports editor of the *New York Press*, because it fit more easily into headlines.

John Mosedale

If you had to limit yourself to one aspect of American life, the showdowns between pitcher and hitter, quarterback and defense, hustler and fish, would tell you more about politics, manners, style in this country than any other one thing. Sports constitute a code, a language of the emotions, and a tourist who skips the stadiums will not recoup his losses at Lincoln Center or Grant's Tomb.

Wilfrid Sheed
author

Yankee Stadium is a law unto itself. . . . I once sneaked out to center field as a youth to see how things looked from Mickey Mantle's point of view and felt the same tingle some people get from Civil War battlefields.

Wilfrid Sheed

The House That Ruth Built.

Fred G. Lieb
legendary sportswriter who coined the timeless nickname in 1923

Gehrig liked to hit in the arena on the east bank of the Harlem River, while Ruth avers he would rather do his hitting almost any place else. Their attitudes toward hitting in the stadium are reflected in the fact that the Babe has hit the majority of his home runs on the road, and Lou has made most of his at home.

New York Sun

Yankee Stadium is the Rolls-Royce of stadiums.

Fernando Ferrer
Bronx Borough president

The old stadium had a biblical look. I assumed it had been standing on 161st Street since before Christ. Years later, when I saw the actual Roman Coliseum, I couldn't suppress an inner gasp of recognition. Ahhh! It's like Yankee Stadium.

Laura Cunningham
author

The stadium was like the Empire State Building or the Grand Canyon of baseball, and every time I stepped inside of it I had to pinch myself!

Mel Allen
nineteen-year radio and television voice of the Yankees

There's the bigness of it. There are those high stands and all the people smoking and, of course, the shadows.

Ted Williams

Yankee Stadium was a mistake. Not mine, but the Giants.

Col. Jacob Ruppert

The stadium is hallowed ground.

Bill Waite
Yankee Stadium employee for more than fifty years

The filigreed gray-green facade above the third tier of the grandstand remains baseball's unscaled peak.

Donald Honig

12

LIFE LESSONS

Don't quit until every base is uphill.
Babe Ruth

There is no greater inspiration to any American boy than Lou Gehrig. For if this awkward, inept, and downright clumsy player that I knew in the beginning could through sheer drive and determination turn himself into the finest first-base-covering machine in all baseball, then nothing is impossible to any man or boy in the country.

Paul Gallico

I always believe that an honest question deserves an honest answer, but sometimes you get into trouble by saying the wrong thing.

Roger Maris

I prayed to my favorite, Saint Jude, as I had done all season. He is the patron saint for lost causes. . . . I had felt all along that Roger's chances of beating the record were nearly hopeless. I prayed the hardest that Roger would be protected from injuries. He had had so many. Above all, I have always prayed for what Roger and I believe in most—to do your level best no matter what you do.

Pat Maris
in the pregame hours, October 1,
1961, the last game of the season,
in which her husband hit his
record-breaking 61st home run

The American people will always admire a man who overcomes great pressures to achieve an outstanding goal.

President John F. Kennedy
in a message to Roger Maris

Ever since I was a kid, I'd had the overpowering feeling that the breaks would never be mine. It was the first time I had come up with the right game in the right place.

Allie "The Chief" Reynolds
pitcher (1947–54)

Reynolds is the only Yankee to hurl two no-hitters (both in 1951). This quote refers to the opening game of the 1949 World Series—a nail-biting 1-0 thriller over the Brooklyn Dodgers that was not settled until Tommy Henrich's bottom-of-the-ninth home run. The victory was a turning point in Reynolds's career.

I admit that in the past I've been cautious about using rookies, but . . . sometimes, a young arm is better than an old head.

Miller Huggins

A team is where a boy can prove his courage on his own. A gang is where a coward goes to hide.

Mickey Mantle

Baseball was my whole life. Nothing was ever as much fun as baseball.

Mickey Mantle, 1988

I could never be a manager. I can't manage myself. What would I do with 25 other problems?

Mickey Mantle

My mom raised me to be independent. She taught me to speak my mind. She believed in me just like I am.

David Wells

Scallions are the greatest cure for a batting slump ever invented.

Babe Ruth

There is nothing so dead as a dead arm.

Bennie Bengough
catcher (1923–30)

Now that I'm coming to the small end of the funnel, I find myself more and more reviewing my life and asking myself whether I'm justified in believing I was a success. I find myself in the quiet of night . . . thinking, "Could I have done this? Could I have done that? Would it have been commensurate with my character to do it?"

Waite Hoyt

Yankees in the Hall of Fame

Year of induction noted in parentheses

Ed Barrow (1953)
Yogi Berra (1970)
Jack Chesbro (1946)
Earle Combs (1970)
Bill Dickey (1954)
Joe DiMaggio (1955)
Whitey Ford (1974)
Lou Gehrig (1939)
Lefty Gómez (1972)
Waite Hoyt (1969)
Miller Huggins (1964)
Jim "Catfish" Hunter
    (1987)

Reggie Jackson (1993)
Willie Keeler (1939)
Tony Lazzeri (1991)
Joe McCarthy (1957)
Larry MacPhail (1978)
Lee MacPhail (1998)
Mickey Mantle (1974)
Herb Pennock (1948)
Phil Rizzuto (1994)
Red Ruffing (1967)
Babe Ruth (1936)
Casey Stengel (1966)
George Weiss (1970)

13

THE SUBWAY SERIES

We are a part of history. We are something special. We were playing for more than the World Series. Now we have some bragging rights.

Bernie Williams
after the 2000 Subway Series, the fourteenth edition between the New York Yankees and New York's National League champion

Almost as long as the Yankees have been playing baseball there has been a Subway Series—that interborough phenomenon that on occasion pits the Pinstripers against a National League champion also from New York City in the World Series.

There have been fourteen of them, from the first Yankees-Giants clash in 1921 through the 2000 edition versus the Mets. The Bronx Bombers have dominated the competition, taking eleven of the fourteen, including nine in a row from 1923–53.

Talk about an inbred Series, all games in the first two Subway Series, in 1921 and '22, were played in the same ballpark—the legendary Polo Grounds, home of the Giants and landlord to the Yankees, who also called Coogan's Bluff home when the Giants were on the road.

The Giants took those first two meetings before finally bowing to the Yanks in 1923, the year the Bombers debuted in their own home park, lavish Yankee Stadium, built just across the Harlem River from the Polo Grounds.

The Giants participated in the first five Subway Series before handing off to the Brooklyn Dodgers, who faced the Yankees in seven of the next eight. The Mets are the third and latest team to join the famous series, and of course, are also the most recent to taste defeat at the hands of New York's perennial champs.

The games were raw, emotional, edgy, a bit dangerous, bizarre, and ultimately tighter than a streetwalker's spandex.

Tom Verducci
Sports Illustrated, October 30, 2000, on the 2000 World Series between the Yankees and the Mets

1921

Spitballer "Shufflin'" Phil Douglas beats the Yankees twice in a thrilling best-of-nine series that sees Giants pitching hold the Yankees to a composite .207 batting average. Babe Ruth, who stunned fans and foes alike that year by recording a stupendous 59 regular-season home runs, is the only Yankee to hit over .300 for the series. The Yankees, behind Carl Mays and ace Waite Hoyt, shutout the Giants in the first two games, but John McGraw's scrappers claw back to take five of the next six. Giants 5-3.

1922

Ruth, who goes just 2-for-17 (.118), is indicative of poor Yankees hitting in general (.203), as the Bombers fail to record a win in a five-game series against the Giants that produces an odd tie. Game 2 is called on account of darkness after ten scoreless innings, and New Yorkers rifle the field with bottles and seat cushions in protest. Like the year before, with all games being played at the Polo Grounds, the Giants and Yankees alternate as home team. Giants 4-0-1.

1923

The Yankees move into their new stadium across the Harlem River, the one that Ruth built. The fabulous stadium brings the Yanks a change in luck, as they gain their first world championship ever—over the New York Giants, their third Subway Series in successive years with John McGraw's men.

Ruth finally breaks out in this World Series, hitting three home runs and batting .368. A Giants outfielder named Casey Stengel helps the Giants to an opening-game win with his inside-the-park homer. Yankees 4-2.

1936

After a thirteen-year hiatus, the Yanks and Giants resume their Subway feud. The Yankees unveil classy rookie Joe DiMaggio to go with sturdy veteran Lou Gehrig. Future immortal Lefty Gómez maintains his unbeaten World Series streak, collecting two series victories, as the Bombers overpower the Giants by scores of 18-4 and 13-5. The Clipper (nine hits) and future Hall of Famer Red Rolfe, along with little-known outfielder Jake Powell, both with ten hits apiece, pace the Yanks' barrage. Yankees 4-2.

1937

In his final World Series as a Yankee, Tony "Poosh 'Em Up" Lazzeri hits .400 to aid an outstanding pitching effort by aces Lefty Gómez and Red Ruffing, who combine to beat the Giants on three complete-game wins. The Yanks, for the second year in a row and for the third straight time in a Subway Series, beat their National League city rivals. Yankees 4-1.

1941

The year of Joe DiMaggio's unparalleled 56-game hitting streak winds up with the first Subway Series encounter against the Bums from Brooklyn. One of baseball's immortal moments occurs in Game 4, with the Dodgers holding a 4-3 edge in the top of the ninth. Dodgers reliever Hugh Casey strikes out Tommy Henrich for the apparent third out and a Brooklyn victory, but catcher Mickey Owen lets the strike-three pitch get away and Henrich reaches first. The Yanks rally for four runs, and the series turns. Instead of being even at two games apiece, it's 3-1 Yanks. They wrap up their ninth world title the next day. Yankees 4-1.

1947

More memorable moments abound as the Yankees' Bill Bevens loses a Game 4 no-hitter with two out in the bottom of the ninth, when Brooklyn pinch hitter Cookie Lavagetto doubles in two runs for a Dodgers victory to even the series. In Game 6, Joe DiMaggio is robbed by little substitute left fielder Joe Gionfriddo of a sure home run, preserving Brooklyn's series-tying win. Still, it's the Yanks who take the seventh and deciding game behind the shutout relief of Bevens and ace Joe Page. The first appearance of an African-American player in a World Series is made by the Dodgers' NL Rookie of the Year, Jackie Robinson. Yankees 4-3.

1949

Again the Dodgers provide the Subway opposition as the Yankees begin their legendary run of five straight world championships. The Bombers hit just .226, but Brooklyn hits worse (.210). Allie "The Chief" Reynolds posts an ERA of 0.00 in 12.1 innings pitched as the Yanks rule in five games. Yankees 4-1.

1951

This postseason is best remembered for a sub-Subway Series before the main event. In a one-game playoff, the Giants' Bobby Thomson hits "The Shot Heard 'Round the World," defeating Brooklyn to advance to the World Series opposite the Yanks.

The real Subway Series isn't nearly as memorable as the National League playoff, but it debuts a young pair of future superstars: the Giants' Willie Mays and the Yankees' Mickey Mantle. It is also the tenth and final World Series for an aging Joe DiMaggio, as well as the beginning of the injury-prone Mantle era. The rookie severely injures his knee in Game 2, playing right field, next to DiMaggio. Yankees 4-2.

1952

The Dodgers take a 3-2 lead back to Ebbets Field, but clutch relief pitching from Allie Reynolds in Games 6 and 7 and critical home runs by Mantle in those two games brings the Bombers their fifteenth world championship. The play of the series is Billy Martin's flying, hats-off, last-second catch of Jackie Robinson's bases-loaded infield pop fly to preserve the Game 7 win. Yankees 4-3.

1953

Billy Martin's heroics continue as the Yanks' second baseman hits .500, including two home runs, two triples, and eight runs batted in. Mickey Mantle contributes a pair of homers, and again Allie Reynolds is expert in relief, as the Bombers blitz Brooklyn. Martin's twelve hits, including the Game 6 series-winner, ensures his selection as MVP. Yankees 4-2.

1955

Salvation comes to Flatbush. The Dodgers finally embrace victory after seven humiliating attempts in World Series play. The Yankees run of nine consecutive Subway Series triumphs ends as unlikely Brooklyn hero, pitcher Johnny Podres, twice beats the Bombers, including the finale in Game 7. The series has some stellar moments, including Jackie Robinson's steal of home in the Bums' Game 1 loss, and Dodgers left fielder Sandy Amoros' foul-line robbery of a sure Yogi Berra opposite-field extra-base hit, with two runners on, to protect Podres's Game 7 win. Brooklyn 4-3.

1956

Another seven-game thriller, a reverse carbon copy of the 1955 series. Every game was won by the team who had lost its equivalent the previous year. The Bombers took the decisive finale, 9-0, behind Johnny Kucks's three-hitter and Yogi Berra's pair of two-run homers. Icing it was Bill "Moose" Skowron's seventh-inning grand slam. The Yankees blast twelve homers in the series, including three each by Berra and Mantle. But the big slice of history is cut by an unassuming New York right-hander named Don Larsen, who in Game 5 throws the one and only perfect game in World Series history. In that same game, Mantle's two-run homer and tremendous running catch of a deep left-center field fly in the fifth support Larsen's gem. Yankees 4-3.

2000

It took forty-four years for the Subway Series to surface once again, but thanks to the Yankees' eleventh-hour awakening from a deadly late-season slumber and the Mets matter-of-fact manhandling of the Giants and Cardinals, the talk turns to the No. 7 and No. 4 trains running those underground labyrinths under the streets of New York City.

It is worth the wait and the hype. The Yankees score nineteen runs, the Mets seventeen. There is the twelve-inning nail-biter that opens the Series and that some say takes the steam out of the Mets. A thrown splintered bat by Roger Clemens in the direction of Mike Piazza, inflaming an old wound that the press makes even more gaping, grabs almost as many headlines as the gem Clemens pitches in Game 2. A rising Yanks superstar at shortstop, Derek Jeter, in the end takes MVP honors for his omnipresent brilliance on the diamond, and lastly, there is of course talk of yet another Yankees dynasty—four world championships in five years.

The only thing token about the Yankees' twenty-sixth championship is the turnstile fare for this fourteenth Subway Series. Yankees 4-1.

THE ELEVEN WORLD SERIES
THAT GOT AWAY

1921	v. New York Giants	5-3
1922	v. New York Giants	4-0
1926	v. St. Louis Cardinals	4-3
1942	v. St. Louis Cardinals	4-1
1955	v. Brooklyn Dodgers	4-3
1957	v. Milwaukee Braves	4-3
1960	v. Pittsburgh Pirates	4-3
1963	v. Los Angeles Dodgers	4-0
1964	v. St. Louis Cardinals	4-3
1976	v. Cincinnati Reds	4-0
1981	v. Los Angeles Dodgers	4-2

14

THE BRONX CLUBHOUSE

Some kids dream of joining the circus, others of becoming a major league baseball player. As a member of the New York Yankees, I've gotten to do both.

Graig Nettles ▪
third baseman (1973–83),
on the Yankees' "Bronx Zoo"
days of the 1970s

PULL UP a stool next to that empty locker over there.

The boys'll be comin' in soon. Looks like ole Casey's brought the beer this time. They'll like that.

Keep your ears open. You'll likely hear a gem or two. Why ole Lefty, he's a regular clown. And the Babe, he'll let out a good one every so often. Course, that Nettles is a ham, too, and you can't hardly keep ole Casey from runnin' his mouth.

I think I hear cleats clattering in the tunnel.

I married him for better or for worse, but not for lunch.

Hazel Weiss
wife of longtime Yankees general manager George Weiss, after experiencing her husband on a daily basis when he was forcibly retired from major league baseball for a year, 1960.

I don't play cards, I don't play golf, and I don't go to the picture show. All that's left is baseball.

Casey Stengel

Outside of baseball, I think Casey loved dancing most.

Edna Stengel

Yankee American League MVPs

1923	Babe Ruth, *right fielder*
1927	Lou Gehrig, *first baseman*
1936	Lou Gehrig, *first baseman*
1939	Joe DiMaggio, *center fielder*
1941	Joe DiMaggio, *center fielder*
1942	Joe Gordon, *second baseman*
1943	Spud Chandler, *pitcher*
1947	Joe DiMaggio, *center fielder*
1950	Phil Rizzuto, *shortstop*
1951	Yogi Berra, *catcher*
1954	Yogi Berra, *catcher*
1955	Yogi Berra, *catcher*
1956	Mickey Mantle, *center fielder*
1957	Mickey Mantle, *center fielder*
1960	Roger Maris, *right fielder*
1961	Roger Maris, *right fielder*
1962	Mickey Mantle, *center fielder*
1963	Elston Howard, *catcher*
1976	Thurman Munson, *catcher*
1985	Don Mattingly, *first baseman*

I was sitting here the other day, and I tried to remember what it was like to hit a home run and win a game. And I couldn't remember. It was like the whole thing happened to somebody else.

Mickey Mantle
on his fiftieth birthday

When I think of all those wasted hours, my God, what somebody with brains could have done with them. You could go to bed at three o'clock in the morning, because you wouldn't have to be out [at the park] until one o'clock. You could sleep until eleven. All those wasted hours.

Mark Koenig

I've often thought that a lot of awards you get are made-up deals so you'll come to the dinners.

Mickey Mantle, 1985

During my 18 years I came to bat almost 10,000 times. I struck out about 1,700 times and walked maybe 1,800 times. You figure a ballplayer will average about 500 at bats a season. That means I played seven years without ever hitting the ball.

Mickey Mantle

Oh, well, you weren't Mickey Mantle then!

Darrell Royal
*legendary University of Texas
head football coach, upon meeting
Mantle for what he thought was
the first time*

Mantle corrected him, saying they had met before, when Mickey was being recruited by University of Oklahoma head coach Bud Wilkinson to play football for OU. Royal, the starting quarterback for the Sooners at the time, was given the task of showing the young Mantle around the campus.

The more we lose, the more [George] Steinbrenner will fly in. And the more he flies, the better the chances of the plane crashing.

Graig Nettles

YANKEE AMERICAN LEAGUE
ROOKIES OF THE YEAR

1951   Gil McDougald, *third baseman*

1954   Bob Grim, *pitcher*

1957   Tony Kubek, *shortstop-outfielder*

1962   Tom Tresh, *shortstop*

1968   Stan Bahnsen, *pitcher*

1970   Thurman Munson, *catcher*

1981   Dave Righetti, *pitcher*

1996   Derek Jeter, *shortstop*

YANKEE AMERICAN LEAGUE
BATTING CHAMPIONS

1924   Babe Ruth

1934   Lou Gehrig

1939   Joe DiMaggio

1940   Joe DiMaggio

1945   George "Snuffy" Stirnweiss

1956   Mickey Mantle

1984   Don Mattingly

1994   Paul O'Neill

1998   Bernie Williams

YANKEE CY YOUNG
AWARD WINNERS

1958	Bob Turley
1961	Whitey Ford
1977	Sparky Lyle
1978	Ron Guidry

YANKEE HOME
RUN KINGS

Wally Pipp 1916, 1917

Babe Ruth 1920, 1921, 1923, 1924, 1926, 1927, 1928, 1929, 1930, 1931

Bob Meusel 1925

Lou Gehrig 1931, 1934, 1936

Joe DiMaggio 1937, 1948

Nick Etten 1944

Mickey Mantle 1955, 1956, 1958, 1960

Roger Maris 1961

Graig Nettles 1976

Reggie Jackson 1980

When I'm not hitting, my wife could pitch and get me out.

Roger Maris

If I'd just tried for them dinky singles, I could've batted around .600.

Babe Ruth

I always had good stuff, only some days it didn't work as well as others.

Allie Reynolds

I've got a new invention. It's a revolving bowl for tired goldfish.

Lefty Gómez

I never had a bad night in my life, but I've had a few bad mornings.

Lefty Gómez

I was supposed to be a doctor. Then a priest. I took a little of each and played baseball.

Joe Torre

YANKEE WORLD SERIES MVPs

1949	Joe Page, *pitcher*
1950	Jerry Coleman, *second baseman*
1951	Phil Rizzuto, *shortstop*
1952	Johnny Mize, *first baseman*
1953	Billy Martin, *second baseman*
1956	Don Larsen, *pitcher*
1958	Elston Howard, *catcher* (Ruth)
	Bob Turley, *pitcher* (Sport)
1960	Bobby Richardson, *second baseman* (Sport)
1961	Whitey Ford, *pitcher*
1962	Ralph Terry, *pitcher*
1977	Reggie Jackson, *outfielder*
1978	Bucky Dent, *shortstop*
1996	Cecil Fielder, *first baseman–dh* (Ruth)
	John Wetteland, *pitcher* (Sport)
1998	Scott Brosius, *third baseman*
1999	Mariano Rivera, *pitcher*
2000	Derek Jeter, *shortstop*

In 1949 the New York chapter of the Baseball Writers' Association of America established the Babe Ruth Award. In 1955 *Sport* magazine introduced the Sport Award. Both recognize the World Series MVP.

Son, it ain't the water cooler that's striking you out.

Casey Stengel
*to a young Mickey Mantle,
who, early in his career, would
periodically vent his frustrations
on the dugout water cooler,
particularly after striking out.*

I hope he watches me and is pulling his hair out of his beard.

Orlando Hernández
on Cuban dictator Fidel Castro

He was my childhood.

Billy Crystal
*actor-comedian, at Mickey
Mantle's funeral*

It's great to be young and a Yankee.

Joe DiMaggio

Babe Ruth's suitcase.

Ping Bodie
*outfielder (1918–21), when asked
who he roomed with when the
Yankees were on the road.*

15

CHAMPIONSHIP LINEUPS

THE 1923 YANKEES

98–54

Miller Huggins, *manager*

Benny Bengough, *catcher*

Joe Bush, *pitcher*

Joe Dugan, *third baseman*

Mike Gazella, *shortstop, second and third baseman*

Lou Gehrig, *first baseman*

Hinkey Haines, *outfielder*

Harvey Hendrick, *outfielder*

Fred Hofmann, *catcher*

Waite Hoyt, *pitcher*

Ernie Johnson, *shortstop and third baseman*

Sam Jones, *pitcher*

Mike McNally, *shortstop, second and third baseman*

Carl Mays, *pitcher*

Bob Meusel, *outfielder*

Herb Pennock, *pitcher*

George Pipgras, *pitcher*

Wally Pipp, *first baseman*

Oscar Roettger, *pitcher*

Babe Ruth, *outfielder and first baseman*

Wally Schang, *catcher*

Everett Scott, *shortstop*

Bob Shawkey, *pitcher*

Elmer Smith, *outfielder*

Aaron Ward, *second baseman*

Whitey Witt, *outfielder*

Starting lineups in **bold**

George Herman "Babe" Ruth

Lou Gehrig

THE 1927 YANKEES

110–44

Miller Huggins, *manager*

Benny Bengough, *catcher*
Pat Collins, *catcher*
Earle Combs, *outfielder*
Joe Dugan, *third baseman*
Cedric Durst, *outfielder and first baseman*
Mike Gazella, *third baseman and shortstop*
Lou Gehrig, *first baseman*
Joe Giard, *pitcher*
Johnny Grabowski, *catcher*
Waite Hoyt, *pitcher*
Mark Koenig, *shortstop*

Tony Lazzeri, *second baseman*
Bob Meusel, *outfielder*
Wilcy Moore, *pitcher*
Ray Morehart, *second baseman*
Ben Paschal, *outfielder*
Herb Pennock, *pitcher*
George Pipgras, *pitcher*
Dutch Ruether, *pitcher*
Babe Ruth, *outfielder*
Bob Shawkey, *pitcher*
Urban Shocker, *pitcher*
Myles Thomas, *pitcher*
Julie Wera, *third baseman*

THE 1928 YANKEES

101–53

Miller Huggins, *manager*

Benny Bengough, *catcher*
George Burns, *first baseman*
Archie Campbell, *pitcher*
Pat Collins, *catcher*
Earle Combs, *outfielder*
Stan Coveleski, *pitcher*
Bill Dickey, *catcher*
Joe Dugan, *third baseman*
Leo Durocher, *shortstop and second baseman*
Cedric Durst, *outfielder and first baseman*
Mike Gazella, *third baseman and shortstop*
Lou Gehrig, *first baseman*
Johnny Grabowski, *catcher*
Fred Heimach, *pitcher*

Waite Hoyt, *pitcher*
Hank Johnson, *pitcher*
Mark Koenig, *shortstop*
Tony Lazzeri, *second baseman*
Bob Meusel, *outfielder*
Wilcy Moore, *pitcher*
Ben Paschal, *outfielder*
Herb Pennock, *pitcher*
George Pipgras, *pitcher*
Gene Robertson, *second and third baseman*
Babe Ruth, *outfielder*
Rosy Ryan, *pitcher*
Al Shealy, *pitcher*
Myles Thomas, *pitcher*
Tom Zachary, *pitcher*

CHAMPIONSHIP LINEUPS

THE 1932 YANKEES

107–47

Joe McCarthy, *manager*

Johnny Allen, *pitcher*
Ivy Andrews, *pitcher*
Sammy Byrd, *outfielder*
Jumbo Brown, *pitcher*
Ben Chapman, *outfielder*
Earle Combs, *outfielder*
Dusty Cooke, *pinch runner*
Frankie Crosetti, *shortstop*
Charlie Devens, *pitcher*
Bill Dickey, *catcher*
Doc Farrell, *infielder*
Lou Gehrig, *first baseman*
Joe Glenn, *catcher*
Lefty Gómez, *pitcher*
Myril Hoag, *outfielder and first baseman*
Hank Johnson, *pitcher*

Art Jorgens, *catcher*
Lyn Lary, *infielder and outfielder*
Tony Lazzeri, *second baseman*
Danny Macfayden, *pitcher*
Wilcy Moore, *pitcher*
Johnny Murphy, *pitcher*
Herb Pennock, *pitcher*
Eddie Phillips, *catcher*
George Pipgras, *pitcher*
Gordon Rhodes, *pitcher*
Red Ruffing, *pitcher*
Babe Ruth, *outfielder*
Jack Saltzgaver, *second baseman*
Roy Schalk, *second baseman*
Joe Sewell, *third baseman*
Ed Wells, *pitcher*

THE 1936 YANKEES

102–51

Joe McCarthy, *manager*

Johnny Broaca, *pitcher*

Jumbo Brown, *pitcher*

Ben Chapman, *outfielder*

Frankie Crosetti, *shortstop*

Bill Dickey, *catcher*

Joe DiMaggio, *outfielder*

Lou Gehrig, *first baseman*

Joe Glenn, *catcher*

Lefty Gómez, *pitcher*

Bump Hadley, *pitcher*

Don Heffner, *shortstop, second and third baseman*

Myril Hoag, *outfielder*

Roy Johnson, *outfielder*

Art Jorgens, *catcher*

Ted Kleinhans, *pitcher*

Tony Lazzeri, *second baseman*

Pat Malone, *pitcher*

Johnny Murphy, *pitcher*

Monte Pearson, *pitcher*

Jake Powell, *outfielder*

Red Rolfe, *third baseman*

Red Ruffing, *pitcher*

Jack Saltzgaver, *infielder*

Bob Seeds, *outfielder and third baseman*

George Selkirk, *outfielder*

Steve Sundra, *pitcher*

Dixie Walker, *outfielder*

Kemp Wicker, *pitcher*

CHAMPIONSHIP LINEUPS

THE 1937 YANKEES

102–52

Joe McCarthy, *manager*

Ivy Andrews, *pitcher*
Johnny Broaca, *pitcher*
Bill Dickey, *catcher*
Spud Chandler, *pitcher*
Frankie Crosetti, *shortstop*
Babe Dahlgren, *pinch runner*
Joe DiMaggio, *outfielder*
Lou Gehrig, *first baseman*
Joe Glenn, *catcher*
Lefty Gómez, *pitcher*
Bump Hadley, *pitcher*
Don Heffner, *infielder*
Tommy Henrich, *outfielder*
Myril Hoag, *outfielder*

Roy Johnson, *outfielder*
Art Jorgens, *catcher*
Tony Lazzeri, *second baseman*
Frank Makosky, *pitcher*
Pat Malone, *pitcher*
Johnny Murphy, *pitcher*
Monte Pearson, *pitcher*
Jake Powell, *outfielder*
Red Rolfe, third baseman
Red Ruffing, *pitcher*
Jack Saltzgaver, *first baseman*
George Selkirk, *outfielder*
Joe Vance, *pitcher*
Kemp Wicker, *pitcher*

THE 1938 YANKEES

99–53

Joe McCarthy, *manager*

Ivy Andrews, *pitcher*
Joe Beggs, *pitcher*
Spud Chandler, *pitcher*
Frankie Crosetti, *shortstop*
Babe Dahlgren, *first and third baseman*
Bill Dickey, *catcher*
Joe DiMaggio, *outfielder*
Atley Donald, *pitcher*
Wes Ferrell, *pitcher*
Lou Gehrig, *first baseman*
Joe Glenn, *catcher*
Lefty Gómez, *pitcher*
Joe Gordon, *second baseman*
Bump Hadley, *pitcher*

Tommy Henrich, *outfielder*
Myril Hoag, *outfielder*
Art Jorgens, *catcher*
Bill Knickerbocker, *second baseman and shortstop*
Johnny Murphy, *pitcher*
Monte Pearson, *pitcher*
Jake Powell, *outfielder*
Red Rolfe, *third baseman*
Red Ruffing, *pitcher*
George Selkirk, *outfielder*
Lee Stine, *pitcher*
Steve Sundra, *pitcher*
Joe Vance, *pitcher*

CHAMPIONSHIP LINEUPS

THE 1939 YANKEES

106–45

Joe McCarthy, manager

Spud Chandler, *pitcher*
Frankie Crosetti, *shortstop*
Babe Dahlgren, *first baseman*
Bill Dickey, *catcher*
Joe DiMaggio, *outfielder*
Atley Donald, *pitcher*
Wes Ferrell, *pitcher*
Joe Gallagher, *outfielder*
Lou Gehrig, *first baseman*
Lefty Gómez, *pitcher*
Joe Gordon, *second baseman*
Bump Hadley, *pitcher*
Tommy Henrich, *outfielder and first baseman*

Oral Hildebrand, *pitcher*
Art Jorgens, *catcher*
Charlie Keller, *outfielder*
Bill Knickerbocker, *second baseman and shortstop*
Johnny Murphy, *pitcher*
Monte Pearson, *pitcher*
Jake Powell, *outfielder*
Red Rolfe, *third baseman*
Buddy Rosar, *catcher*
Red Ruffing, *pitcher*
Marius Russo, *pitcher*
George Selkirk, *outfielder*
Steve Sundra, *pitcher*

THE 1941 YANKEES

101–53

Joe McCarthy, *manager*

Tiny Bonham, *pitcher*
Frenchy Bordagaray, *outfielder*
Norm Branch, *pitcher*
Marv Breuer, *pitcher*
Spud Chandler, *pitcher*
Frankie Crosetti, *shortstop and third baseman*
Bill Dickey, *catcher*
Joe DiMaggio, *outfielder*
Atley Donald, *pitcher*
Lefty Gómez, *pitcher*
Joe Gordon, *second baseman*
Tommy Henrich, *outfielder*
Charlie Keller, *outfielder*

Johnny Lindell, *pinch hitter*
Johnny Murphy, *pitcher*
Steve Peek, *pitcher*
Jerry Priddy, *infielder*
Phil Rizzuto, *shortstop*
Red Rolfe, *third baseman*
Buddy Rosar, *catcher*
Red Ruffing, *pitcher*
Marius Russo, *pitcher*
George Selkirk, *outfielder*
Ken Silvestri, *catcher*
Charley Stanceu, *pitcher*
Johnny Sturm, *first baseman*
George Washburn, *pitcher*

CHAMPIONSHIP LINEUPS

THE 1943 YANKEES

98–56

Joe McCarthy, *manager*

Tiny Bonham, *pitcher*
Hank Borowy, *pitcher*
Marv Breuer, *pitcher*
Tommy Byrne, *pitcher*
Spud Chandler, *pitcher*
Frankie Crosetti, *shortstop*
Bill Dickey, *catcher*
Atley Donald, *pitcher*
Nick Etten, *first baseman*
Joe Gordon, *second baseman*
Oscar Grimes, *shortstop and first baseman*
Rollie Hemsley, *catcher*
Billy Johnson, *third baseman*

Charlie Keller, *outfielder*
Johnny Lindell, *outfielder*
Bud Metheny, *outfielder*
Johnny Murphy, *pitcher*
Aaron Robinson, *pinch hitter*
Marius Russo, *pitcher*
Ken Sears, *catcher*
Tuck Stainback, *outfielder*
Snuffy Stirnweiss, *shortstop and second baseman*
Jim Turner, *pitcher*
Roy Weatherly, *outfielder*
Butch Wensloff, *pitcher*
Bill Zuber, *pitcher*

THE 1947 YANKEES

97–57

Bucky Harris, *manager*

Yogi Berra, *catcher and outfielder*

Bill Bevens, *pitcher*

Bobby Brown, *third baseman, shortstop, and outfielder*

Tommy Byrne, *pitcher*

Spud Chandler, *pitcher*

Allie Clark, *outfielder*

Frank Colman, *outfielder*

Frankie Crosetti, *second baseman and shortstop*

Joe DiMaggio, *outfielder*

Karl Drews, *pitcher*

Lonny Frey, *second baseman*

Randy Gumpert, *pitcher*

Tommy Henrich, *outfielder*

Ralph Houk, *catcher*

Billy Johnson, *third baseman*

Don Johnson, *pitcher*

Charlie Keller, *outfielder*

Johnny Lindell, *outfielder*

Sherm Lollar, *catcher*

Johnny Lucadello, *second baseman*

Al Lyons, *pitcher*

George McQuinn, *first baseman*

Bobo Newsom, *pitcher*

Joe Page, *pitcher*

Jack Phillips, *first baseman*

Mel Queen, *pitcher*

Vic Raschi, *pitcher*

Allie Reynolds, *pitcher*

Phil Rizzuto, *shortstop*

Aaron Robinson, *catcher*

Ted Sepkowski, *pinch runner*

Spec Shea, *pitcher*

Ken Silvestri, *catcher*

Dick Starr, *pitcher*

Snuffy Stirnweiss, *second baseman*

Butch Wensloff, *pitcher*

Bill Wight, *pitcher*

CHAMPIONSHIP LINEUPS

THE 1949 YANKEES

97–57

Casey Stengel, *manager*

Hank Bauer, *outfielder*
Yogi Berra, *catcher*
Bobby Brown, *third baseman*
Ralph Buxton, *pitcher*
Tommy Byrne, *pitcher*
Hugh Casey, *pitcher*
Jerry Coleman, *second baseman*
Joe Collins, *first baseman*
Jim Delsing, *outfielder*
Joe DiMaggio, *outfielder*
Tommy Henrich, *first baseman*
Frank Hiller, *pitcher*
Ralph Houk, *catcher*
Billy Johnson, *infielder*
Charlie Keller, *outfielder*
Dick Kryhoski, *first baseman*
Johnny Lindell, *outfielder*
Ed Lopat, *pitcher*
Cliff Mapes, *outfielder*

Cuddles Marshall, *pitcher*
Johnny Mize, *first baseman*
Fenton Mole, *first baseman*
Gus Niarhos, *catcher*
Joe Page, *pitcher*
Jack Phillips, *first baseman*
Duane Pillette, *pitcher*
Bob Porterfield, *pitcher*
Vic Raschi, *pitcher*
Allie Reynolds, *pitcher*
Phil Rizzuto, *shortstop*
Fred Sanford, *pitcher*
Spec Shea, *pitcher*
Charlie Silvera, *catcher*
Snuffy Stirnweiss, *second and third baseman*
Mickey Witek, *pinch hitter*
Gene Woodling, *outfielder*

Joe DiMaggio

THE 1950 YANKEES

98—56

Casey Stengel, *manager*

Hank Bauer, *outfielder*
Yogi Berra, *catcher*
Bobby Brown, *third baseman*
Tommy Byrne, *pitcher*
Jerry Coleman, *second baseman*
Joe Collins, *first baseman*
Jim Delsing, *pinch hitter*
Joe DiMaggio, *outfielder*
Tom Ferrick, *pitcher*
Whitey Ford, *pitcher*
Tommy Henrich, *first baseman*
Johnny Hopp, *first baseman and outfielder*
Ralph Houk, *catcher*
Jackie Jensen, *outfielder*
Billy Johnson, *third baseman*
Don Johnson, *pitcher*
Johnny Lindell, *outfielder*
Ed Lopat, *pitcher*

Dave Madison, *pitcher*
Cliff Mapes, *outfielder*
Billy Martin, *second and third baseman*
Johnny Mize, *first baseman*
Ernie Nevel, *pitcher*
Joe Ostrowski, *pitcher*
Joe Page, *pitcher*
Bob Porterfield, *pitcher*
Vic Raschi, *pitcher*
Allie Reynolds, *pitcher*
Phil Rizzuto, *shortstop*
Fred Sanford, *pitcher*
Charlie Silvera, *catcher*
Snuffy Stirnweiss, *second baseman*
Dick Wakefield, *pinch hitter*
Gene Woodling, *outfielder*
Hank Workman, *first baseman*

THE 1951 YANKEES

98–56

Casey Stengel, *manager*

Hank Bauer, *outfielder*
Yogi Berra, *catcher*
Jim Brideweser, *shortstop*
Bobby Brown, *third baseman*
Tommy Byrne, *pitcher*
Bob Cerv, *outfielder*
Jerry Coleman, *second baseman*
Joe Collins, *first baseman*
Clint Courtney, *catcher*
Joe DiMaggio, *outfielder*
Tom Ferrick, *pitcher*
Johnny Hopp, *first baseman*
Ralph Houk, *catcher*
Jackie Jensen, *outfielder*
Billy Johnson, *third baseman*
Jack Kramer, *pitcher*
Bob Kuzava, *pitcher*
Ed Lopat, *pitcher*
Gil McDougald, *second and third baseman*
Mickey Mantle, *outfielder*

Cliff Mapes, *outfielder*
Billy Martin, *outfielder, shortstop, second and third baseman*
Johnny Mize, *first baseman*
Tom Morgan, *pitcher*
Ernie Nevel, *pitcher*
Joe Ostrowski, *pitcher*
Stubby Overmire, *pitcher*
Vic Raschi, *pitcher*
Allie Reynolds, *pitcher*
Phil Rizzuto, *shortstop*
Johnny Sain, *pitcher*
Fred Sanford, *pitcher*
Art Schallock, *pitcher*
Spec Shea, *pitcher*
Charlie Silvera, *catcher*
Bob Wiesler, *pitcher*
Archie Wilson, *outfielder*
Gene Woodling, *outfielder*

Yogi Berra

THE 1952 YANKEES

95–59

Casey Stengel, *manager*

Loren Babe, *third baseman*
Hank Bauer, *outfielder*
Yogi Berra, *catcher*
Ewell Blackwell, *pitcher*
Jim Brideweser, *shortstop and second and third baseman*
Bobby Brown, *third baseman*
Andy Carey, *third baseman and shortstop*
Bob Cerv, *outfielder*
Jerry Coleman, *second baseman*
Joe Collins, *first baseman*
Tom Gorman, *pitcher*
Bobby Hogue, *pitcher*
Johnny Hopp, *first baseman*
Ralph Houk, *catcher*
Jackie Jensen, *outfielder*
Charlie Keller, *outfielder*
Bob Kuzava, *pitcher*
Ed Lopat, *pitcher*
Jim McDonald, *pitcher*

Gil McDougald, *third baseman*
Mickey Mantle, *outfielder*
Billy Martin, *second baseman*
Bill Miller, *pitcher*
Johnny Mize, *first baseman*
Tom Morgan, *pitcher*
Irv Noren, *first baseman and outfielder*
Joe Ostrowski, *pitcher*
Vic Raschi, *pitcher*
Allie Reynolds, *pitcher*
Phil Rizzuto, *shortstop*
Johnny Sain, *pitcher*
Ray Scarborough, *pitcher*
Harry Schaeffer, *pitcher*
Johnny Schmitz, *pitcher*
Kal Segrist, *second and third baseman*
Charlie Silvera, *catcher*
Archie Wilson, *pinch hitter*
Gene Woodling, *outfielder*

CHAMPIONSHIP LINEUPS

THE 1953 YANKEES

99–52

Casey Stengel, *manager*

Loren Babe, *third baseman*
Hank Bauer, *outfielder*
Yogi Berra, *catcher*
Ewell Blackwell, *pitcher*
Don Bollweg, *first baseman*
Jim Brideweser, *shortstop*
Andy Carey, *second and third baseman and shortstop*
Bob Cerv, *pinch hitter*
Jerry Coleman, *second baseman and shortstop*
Joe Collins, *first baseman*
Whitey Ford, *pitcher*
Tom Gorman, *pitcher*
Ralph Houk, *catcher*
Steve Kraly, *pitcher*
Bob Kuzava, *pitcher*
Ed Lopat, *pitcher*
Jim McDonald, *pitcher*
Gil McDougald, *third baseman*

Mickey Mantle, *outfielder*
Billy Martin, *second baseman*
Bill Miller, *pitcher*
Willy Miranda, *shortstop*
Johnny Mize, *first baseman*
Irv Noren, *outfielder*
Vic Raschi, *pitcher*
Bill Renna, *outfielder*
Allie Reynolds, *pitcher*
Phil Rizzuto, *shortstop*
Johnny Sain, *pitcher*
Ray Scarborough, *pitcher*
Art Schallock, *pitcher*
Art Schult, *pinch runner*
Charlie Silvera, *catcher and third baseman*
Gus Triandos, *first baseman and catcher*
Gene Woodling, *outfielder*

THE 1956 YANKEES

97–57

Casey Stengel, *manager*

Hank Bauer, *outfielder*
Yogi Berra, *catcher*
Tommy Byrne, *pitcher*
Andy Carey, *third baseman*
Tom Carroll, *third baseman*
Bob Cerv, *outfielder*
Jerry Coleman, *shortstop and second and third baseman*
Rip Coleman, *pitcher*
Joe Collins, *first baseman and outfielder*
Sonny Dixon, *pitcher*
Whitey Ford, *pitcher*
Bob Grim, *pitcher*
Elston Howard, *outfielder*
Billy Hunter, *shortstop and third baseman*
Jim Konstanty, *pitcher*
Johnny Kucks, *pitcher*
Don Larsen, *pitcher*
Jerry Lumpe, *shortstop and third baseman*

Mickey McDermott, *pitcher*
Mickey Mantle, *outfielder*
Billy Martin, *second baseman*
Gil McDougald, *shortstop*
Tom Morgan, *pitcher*
Irv Noren, *outfielder and first baseman*
Bobby Richardson, *second baseman*
Phil Rizzuto, *shortstop*
Eddie Robinson, *first baseman*
Norm Siebern, *outfielder*
Charlie Silvera, *catcher*
Lou Skizas, *pinch hitter*
Bill Skowron, *first baseman*
Enos Slaughter, *outfielder*
Gerry Staley, *pitcher*
Tom Sturdivant, *pitcher*
Ralph Terry, *pitcher*
Bob Turley, *pitcher*
George Wilson, *outfielder*

CHAMPIONSHIP LINEUPS

THE 1958 YANKEES

92–62

Casey Stengel, *manager*

Hank Bauer, *outfielder*
Yogi Berra, *catcher and outfielder*
Andy Carey, *third baseman*
Bobby Delgreco, *outfielder*
Murry Dickson, *pitcher*
Art Ditmar, *pitcher*
Ryne Duren, *pitcher*
Whitey Ford, *pitcher*
Bob Grim, *pitcher*
Elston Howard, *catcher and outfielder*
Johnny James, *pitcher*
Darrell Johnson, *catcher*
Tony Kubek, *shortstop*
Johnny Kucks, *pitcher*
Don Larsen, *pitcher*
Jerry Lumpe, *third baseman and shortstop*

Gil McDougald, *second baseman*
Duke Maas, *pitcher*
Sal Maglie, *pitcher*
Mickey Mantle, *outfielder*
Zach Monroe, *pitcher*
Bobby Richardson, *second and third baseman and shortstop*
Bobby Shantz, *pitcher*
Norm Siebern, *outfielder*
Harry Simpson, *outfielder*
Bill Skowron, *first baseman*
Enos Slaughter, *outfielder*
Tom Sturdivant, *pitcher*
Marv Throneberry, *first baseman and outfielder*
Virgil Trucks, *pitcher*
Bob Turley, *pitcher*

THE 1961 YANKEES

109–53

Ralph Houk, *manager*

Luis Arroyo, *pitcher*
Yogi Berra, *outfielder*
Johnny Blanchard, *catcher*
Clete Boyer, *third baseman*
Bob Cerv, *outfielder*
Tex Clevenger, *pitcher*
Jim Coates, *pitcher*
Bud Daley, *pitcher*
Joe Demaestri, *shortstop*
Art Ditmar, *pitcher*
Al Downing, *pitcher*
Whitey Ford, *pitcher*
Billy Gardner, *third baseman*
Jesse Gonder, *pinch hitter*
Bob Hale, *first baseman*
Elston Howard, *catcher*
Deron Johnson, *third baseman*

Tony Kubek, *shortstop*
Hector Lopez, *outfielder*
Danny McDevitt, *pitcher*
Mickey Mantle, *outfielder*
Roger Maris, *outfielder*
Jack Reed, *outfielder*
Hal Reniff, *pitcher*
Bobby Richardson, *second baseman*
Rollie Sheldon, *pitcher*
Bill Skowron, *first baseman*
Bill Stafford, *pitcher*
Ralph Terry, *pitcher*
Lee Thomas, *pinch hitter*
Earl Torgeson, *first baseman*
Tom Tresh, *shortstop*
Bob Turley, *pitcher*

CHAMPIONSHIP LINEUPS

THE 1962 YANKEES

96–66

Ralph Houk, *manager*

Luis Arroyo, *pitcher*
Johnny Blanchard, *outfielder and catcher*
Yogi Berra, *catcher*
Jim Bouton, *pitcher*
Clete Boyer, *third baseman*
Marshall Bridges, *pitcher*
Hal Brown, *pitcher*
Bob Cerv, *outfielder*
Tex Clevenger, *pitcher*
Jim Coates, *pitcher*
Bud Daley, *pitcher*
Whitey Ford, *pitcher*
Billy Gardner, *second and third baseman*
Jake Gibbs, *third baseman*
Elston Howard, *catcher*

Tony Kubek, *shortstop and outfielder*
Phil Linz, *shortstop*
Dale Long, *first baseman*
Hector Lopez, *outfielder*
Mickey Mantle, *outfielder*
Roger Maris, *outfielder*
Joe Pepitone, *outfielder*
Jack Reed, *outfielder*
Bobby Richardson, *second baseman*
Rollie Sheldon, *pitcher*
Bill Skowron, *first baseman*
Bill Stafford, *pitcher*
Ralph Terry, *pitcher*
Tom Tresh, *shortstop*
Bob Turley, *pitcher*

Graig Nettles

CHAMPIONSHIP LINEUPS

THE 1977 YANKEES

100–62

Billy Martin, *manager*

Dell Alston, *outfielder*

Dave Bergman, *outfielder*

Paul Blair, *outfielder*

Chris Chambliss, *first baseman*

Ken Clay, *pitcher*

Bucky Dent, *shortstop*

Dock Ellis, *pitcher*

Ed Figueroa, *pitcher*

Ron Guidry, *pitcher*

Don Gullett, *pitcher*

Fran Healy, *catcher*

Ellie Hendricks, *catcher*

Ken Holtzman, *pitcher*

Catfish Hunter, *pitcher*

Reggie Jackson, *outfielder*

Cliff Johnson, *catcher*

Dave Kingman, *designated hitter*

Mickey Klutts, *third baseman*

Gene Locklear, *outfielder*

Sparky Lyle, *pitcher*

Larry McCall, *pitcher*

Carlos May, *outfielder*

Thurman Munson, *catcher*

Graig Nettles, *third baseman*

Gil Patterson, *pitcher*

Marty Perez, *third baseman*

Lou Piniella, *designated hitter*

Willie Randolph, *second baseman*

Mickey Rivers, *outfielder*

Fred Stanley, *shortstop*

Stan Thomas, *pitcher*

Dick Tidrow, *pitcher*

Mike Torrez, *pitcher*

Roy White, *outfielder*

Jim Wynn, *outfielder*

George Zeber, *second baseman*

THE 1978 YANKEES

100–63

Billy Martin, Dick Howser, and Bob Lemon, *managers*

Dell Alston, *pinch hitter*
Jim Beattie, *pitcher*
Paul Blair, *outfielder*
Chris Chambliss, *first baseman*
Ken Clay, *pitcher*
Bucky Dent, *shortstop*
Brian Doyle, *second baseman*
Rawly Eastwick, *pitcher*
Ed Figueroa, *pitcher*
Damaso Garcia, *second baseman*
Rich Gossage, *pitcher*
Ron Guidry, *pitcher*
Don Gullett, *pitcher*
Fran Healy, *catcher*
Mike Heath, *catcher*
Ken Holzman, *pitcher*
Catfish Hunter, *pitcher*
Reggie Jackson, *outfielder*
Cliff Johnson, *designated hitter*

Jay Johnstone, *outfielder*
Bob Kammeyer, *pitcher*
Mickey Klutts, *third baseman*
Paul Lindblad, *pitcher*
Sparky Lyle, *pitcher*
Larry McCall, *pitcher*
Andy Messersmith, *pitcher*
Thurman Munson, *catcher*
Graig Nettles, *third baseman*
Lou Piniella, *outfielder*
Willie Randolph, *second baseman*
Mickey Rivers, *outfielder*
Dennis Sherrill, *third baseman*
Jim Spencer, *designated hitter*
Fred Stanley, *shortstop*
Gary Thomasson, *outfielder*
Dick Tidrow, *pitcher*
Roy White, *designated hitter*
George Zeber, *second baseman*

CHAMPIONSHIP LINEUPS

THE 1996 YANKEES

92–70

Joe Torre, *manager*

Mike Aldrete, *outfielder*
Wade Boggs, *third baseman*
David Cone, *pitcher*
Mariano Duncan, *second baseman*
Robert Eenhoorn, *first baseman*
Cecil Fielder, *designated hitter*
Andy Fox, *second baseman*
Joe Girardi, *catcher*
Dwight Gooden, *pitcher*
Charlie Hayes, *third baseman*
Matt Howard, *second baseman*
Dion James, *outfielder*
Derek Jeter, *shortstop*
Pat Kelly, *second baseman*
Jimmy Key, *pitcher*
Jim Leyritz, *catcher*
Matt Luke, *designated hitter*

Tim McIntosh, *catcher*
Tino Martinez, *first baseman*
Ramiro Mendoza, *pitcher*
Jeff Nelson, *pitcher*
Paul O'Neill, *outfielder*
Andy Pettitte, *pitcher*
Jorge Posada, *catcher*
Tim Raines, *outfielder*
Mariano Rivera, *pitcher*
Ruben Rivera, *outfielder*
Kenny Rogers, *pitcher*
Ruben Sierra, *designated hitter*
Luis Sojo, *second baseman*
Darryl Strawberry, *outfielder*
John Wetteland, *pitcher*
Bob Wickman, *pitcher*
Bernie Williams, *outfielder*
Gerald Williams, *outfielder*

THE 1998 YANKEES

114–48

Joe Torre, *manager*

Scott Brosius, *third baseman*

Homer Bush, *second baseman*

David Cone, *pitcher*

Chad Curtis, *outfielder*

Chili Davis, *designated hitter*

Mike Figga, *catcher*

Joe Girardi, *catcher*

Orlando Hernández, *pitcher*

Hideki Irabu, *pitcher*

Derek Jeter, *shortstop*

Chuck Knoblauch, *second baseman*

Ricky Ledee, *outfielder*

Mike Lowell, *third baseman*

Tino Martinez, *first baseman*

Ramiro Mendoza, *pitcher*

Jeff Nelson, *pitcher*

Paul O'Neill, *outfielder*

Andy Pettitte, *pitcher*

Jorge Posada, *catcher*

Tim Raines, *outfielder*

Luis Sojo, *infielder*

Shane Spencer, *outfielder*

Mike Stanton, *pitcher*

Darryl Strawberry, *outfielder*

Dale Sveum, *first baseman*

David Wells, *pitcher*

Bernie Williams, *outfielder*

CHAMPIONSHIP LINEUPS

THE 1999 YANKEES

98–64

Joe Torre, *manager*

Clay Bellinger, *infielder-outfielder*
Scott Brosius, *third baseman*
Roger Clemens, *pitcher*
David Cone, *pitcher*
Chad Curtis, *outfielder*
Chili Davis, *designated hitter*
Joe Girardi, *catcher*
Orlando Hernández, *pitcher*
Hideki Irabu, *pitcher*
Derek Jeter, *shortstop*
D'Angelo Jimenez, *third baseman*
Chuck Knoblauch, *second baseman*

Ricky Ledee, *outfielder*
Jim Leyritz, *catcher*
Jeff Manto, *third baseman*
Tino Martinez, *first baseman*
Paul O'Neill, *outfielder*
Andy Pettitte, *pitcher*
Jorge Posada, *catcher*
Luis Sojo, *infielder*
Alfonso Soriano, *shortstop*
Shane Spencer, *outfielder*
Mike Stanton, *pitcher*
Darryl Strawberry, *outfielder*
Tony Tarasco, *outfielder*
Bernie Williams, *outfielder*

THE 2000 YANKEES

87–74

Joe Torre, *manager*

Clay Bellinger, *outfielder*
Scott Brosius, *third baseman*
Jose Canseco, *outfielder*
Roger Clemens, *pitcher*
David Cone, *pitcher*
Wilson Delgado, *second baseman*
Todd Erdos, *pitcher*
Dwight Gooden, *pitcher*
Jason Grimsley, *pitcher*
Orlando Hernández, *pitcher*
Glenallen Hill, *outfielder*
Derek Jeter, *shortstop*
Lance Johnson, *outfielder*
Felix Jose, *outfielder*
David Justice, *outfielder*
Roberto Kelly, *outfielder*
Chuck Knoblauch, *second baseman*

Ricky Ledee, *outfielder*
Jim Leyritz, *catcher*
Tino Martinez, *first baseman*
Jeff Nelson, *pitcher*
Paul O'Neill, *outfielder*
Andy Pettitte, *pitcher*
Luis Polonia, *outfielder*
Jorge Posada, *catcher*
Luis Sojo, *infielder*
Alfonso Soriano, *shortstop*
Shane Spencer, *outfielder*
Mike Stanton, *pitcher*
Ryan Thompson, *outfielder*
Chris Turner, *catcher*
Jose Vizcaino, *infielder*
Bernie Williams, *outfielder*

BIBLIOGRAPHY

Allen, Maury. *You Could Look It Up: The Life of Casey Stengel.* New York: Times Books, 1979.

Anderson, Dave et al. *The Yankees: The Four Fabulous Eras of Baseball's Most Famous Team.* New York: Random House, 1979.

Auchincloss, Kenneth. "Play Ball." *Newsweek,* October 30, 2000, 63.

Berra, Yogi. *The Yogi Book: "I Really Didn't Say Everything I Said!"* New York: Workman Publishing, 1998.

Blatt, Howard. *This Championship Season.* New York: Simon & Schuster, 1998.

Dame, Kevin T. *Yankee Stadium in Your Pocket.* Charlottesville, Va.: Baseball Direct, 1999.

David, Jay. *The New York Yankees: Legendary Heroes, Magical Moments, and Amazing Stats Through the Decades.* New York: Morrow and Co., 1997.

Hageman, William, and Warren Wilbert. *New York Yankees: Seasons of Glory.* Middle Village, N.Y.: Jonathan David Publishers, 1999.

Halberstam, David. *Summer of '49.* New York: Morrow and Co., 1989.

Herskowitz. Mickey. *Mickey Mantle: An Appreciation.* New York: Morrow and Co., 1995.

Honig, Donald. *Classic Baseball Photographs, 1869–1947.* New York: Smithmark, 1999.

————. *Mays, Mantle, Snider: A Celebration*. New York: Macmillan, 1987.

Mantle, Mickey, and Phil Pepe. *Mickey Mantle: My Favorite Summer, 1956*. New York: Doubleday, 1991.

Mosedale, John. *The Greatest of All: The 1927 New York Yankees*. New York: Dial Press, 1974.

Pepe, Phil. *The Yankees: An Authorized History of the New York Yankees*. 3d Edition. Dallas, Tex.: Taylor, 1998.

Peyer, Tom, and Hart Seely, ed. *O Holy Cow! The Selected Verse of Phil Rizzuto*. Hopewell, N.J.: Ecco Press, 1993.

Robinson, Ray, and Christopher Jennison. *Yankee Stadium: 75 Years of Drama, Glamor, and Glory*. New York: Penguin Studio, 1998.

Rosenfeld, Harvey. *Roger Maris: A Title to Fame*. Fargo, N.D.: Prairie House, 1991.

Ross, Alan. *Echoes from the Ball Park*. Nashville, Tenn.: Walnut Grove Press, 1999.

Ruth, George Herman. *Babe Ruth's Own Book of Baseball*. New York: Putnam, 1928.

Saraceno, Jon. "Yankees Show How Pros Do Job." *USA Today*, October 27, 2000, 3C.

Thorn, John et al. *Total Baseball: The Official Encyclopedia of Major League Baseball*. New York: Viking Penguin, 1997.

Tullius, John. *I'd Rather Be a Yankee*. New York: Macmillan, 1986.

Vanderberg, Bob. *Minnie and the Mick*. South Bend, Ind.: Diamond Communications, 1996.

Verducci, Tom. "Roger & Out" *Sports Illustrated*, October 30, 2000, 42.

Wheeler, Lonnie. *The Official Baseball Hall of Fame Story of Mickey Mantle*. New York: Simon & Schuster, 1990.

INDEX

INDEX

INDEX